P9-BZQ-933

SANTA'S FLIGHT MAP
FOUND IN NORWAY
1654

SANTA EVIDENCE COLLECTION #13.1147

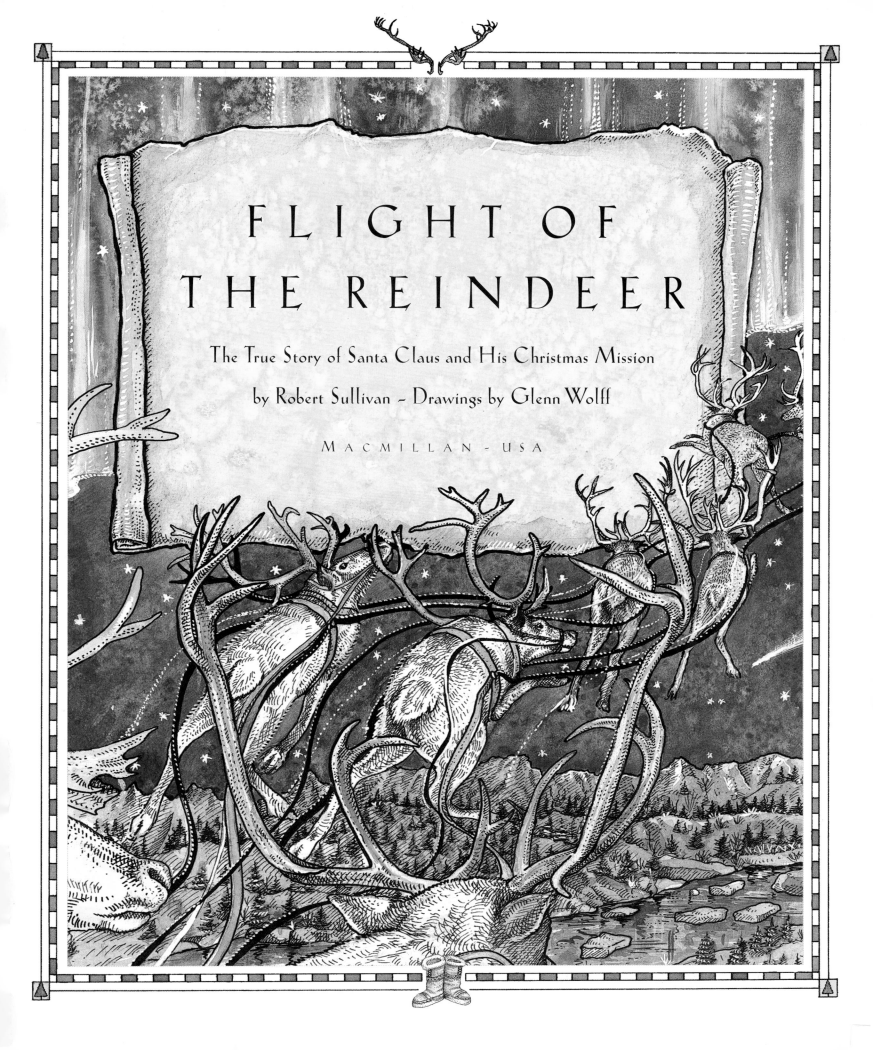

FLIGHT OF THE REINDEER

The True Story of Santa Claus and His Christmas Mission

by Robert Sullivan ~ Drawings by Glenn Wolff

MACMILLAN - USA

Book design by J Porter

Assistant Art Director: Doreen Means

Technical Advisor: David Ziarnowski

Photo Editor: Adrienne Aurichio

Copyright © 1996 by Macmillan, Inc.

All rights reserved. No part of this book may be reproduced or transmitted in any form or by any means, electronic or mechanical, including photocopying, recording, or any information storage and retrieval system, without permission in writing from the Publisher.

Macmillan is a registered trademark of Macmillan, Inc.

Macmillan
A Simon & Schuster Macmillan Company
1633 Broadway, New York, NY 10019

Library of Congress Cataloging-in-Pubication Data
Sullivan, Robert, 1953–
Flight of the reindeer: the true story of Santa Claus
and his Christmas mission / Robert Sullivan. –1st ed.
p.   cm.
ISBN 0-02-861292-2
1. Santa Claus. 2. Christmas. I. Title.
GT4992.S85 1996
394.2'663—dc20   96-14229
CIP

Manufactured in the United States of America
10 9 8 7 6 5 4 3 2 1

Dedication

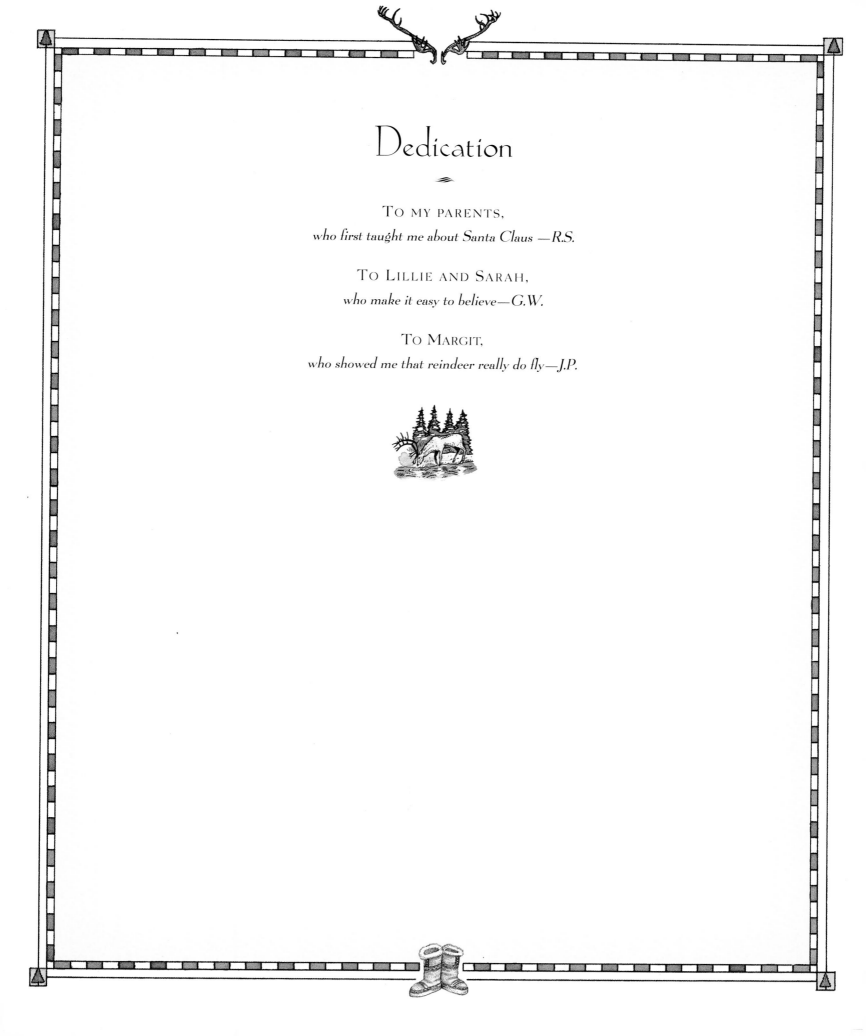

To my parents,
who first taught me about Santa Claus —R.S.

To Lillie and Sarah,
who make it easy to believe—G.W.

To Margit,
who showed me that reindeer really do fly—J.P.

Acknowledgments

DEEPEST THANKS AND BEST CHRISTMAS WISHES are extended to my partners, artist Glenn Wolff and designer J Porter. Merry Christmases go, as well, to the experts and Helpers who shared their knowledge regarding The Mission. Special appreciation is extended to literary agent Jeannie Hanson, and to our talented and sympathetic editor at Macmillan, John Michel. The author, illustrator and designer would like to acknowledge the patience, support and inspiration afforded by their wives while they were off chasing reindeer. They would also like to recognize assistance graciously given by the following individuals and institutions: Doreen Means; Adrienne Aurichio; Dave Ziarnowski; Hank Dempsey; The Potter Park Zoo in Lansing, Michigan; the Michigan State University Museum; Baker Library and the Institute of Arctic Studies at Dartmouth College; The Roger Williams Park Zoo in Providence, Rhode Island; Joe Mehling; Jim Brandenburg; Doug Mindell; Tim Hanrahan; Erick Ingraham;Tonia Means; Craig Neff; the Grose family; Doug Meyerhoff, Paul Traudt, Mary Anne Spiezio and Quad Graphics.

Final thanks to Dan Okrent and all colleagues at LIFE magazine for allowing the time to pursue this project.—R.S.

Table of Contents

COVER PHOTOGRAPH: *The famous "Stark Image," taken
by William H. Johnson in northern New Hampshire in 1993*

FLIGHT OF
THE REINDEER

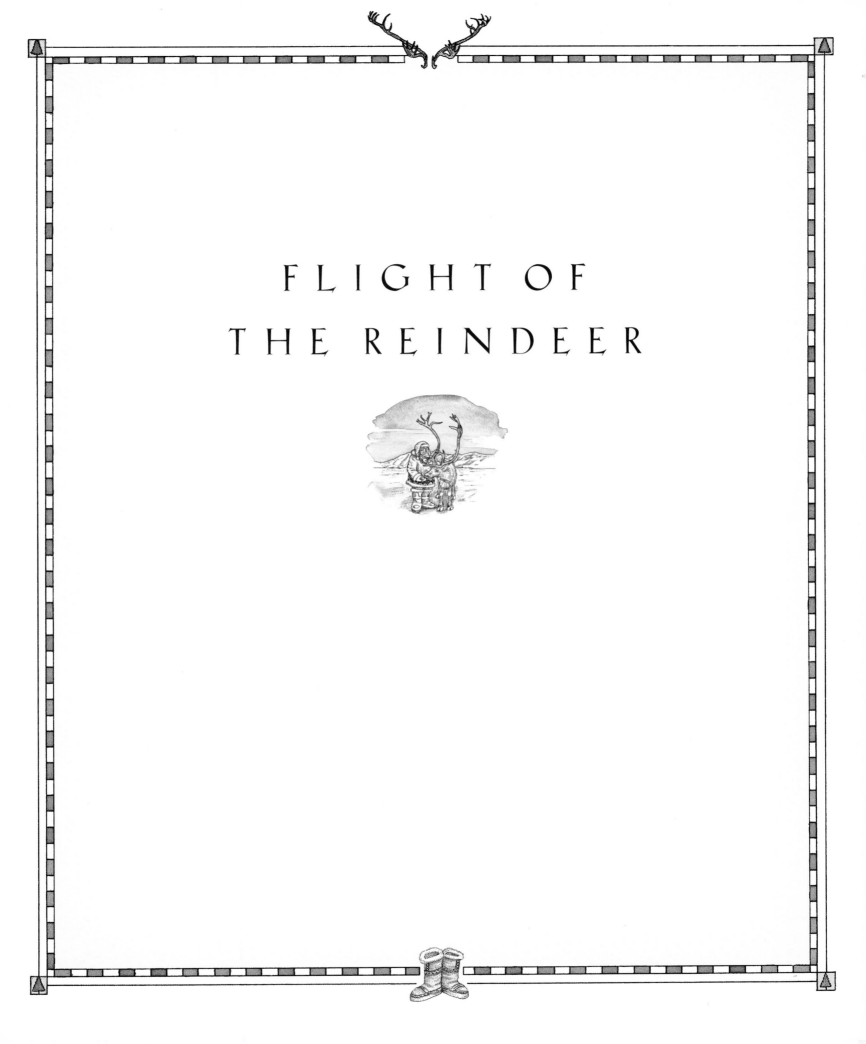

The Reindeer by the River

It Was a Wondrous Thing

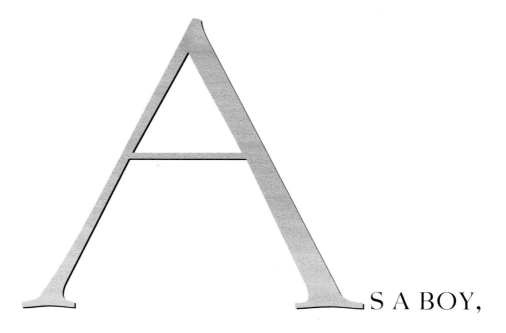

AS A BOY, I knew with certainty that reindeer could fly. As I grew older, I had my doubts. But now—matured and sound of mind—I know again that reindeer can fly. Surely, it is strange. It is strange and marvelous and altogether phenomenal that these deer can spring from the earth and, snouts high and antlers back, mount to the sky.

IT SEEMS NOTHING SHORT OF MIRACULOUS, but miracles do happen, and that this miracle serves mankind at Christmas seems to lend it all some sense. Reindeer do fly. Many have seen it happen, and you yourself may one day.

I have seen it happen—once. I think I may have seen it happen twice.

I grew up in New England in a time when our country-side filled with snow each winter, when the golds and reds of autumn always, *always* yielded to an ice-blue, frosted-windows tableau. The snow would be ankle deep, then knee deep, then hip deep, ever deeper, deeper, deeper. It doesn't snow like that anymore, not most years.

I loved the winter, and I loved snow. I was an all-afternoon sledder as a kid, schussing the hillsides in back of our old white-clapboard house until each evening's sun had set. Then I would trudge home with my trailing sled, heading for the yellow warmth of the distant kitchen. In the finger-aching cold of five o'clock, I felt most alive. My mind would race, and I found myself wondering about all sorts of things.

Are all snowflakes truly unalike? Is there even more snow farther north? What's it like at the North Pole?

Towards December I would wonder as any kid wonders: Do reindeer really fly?

One evening, making my way slowly home after an exhausting session of sledding, I saw something undeniably unusual. It was awfully cold, and the northern lights were at play. Suddenly, silhouetted against those greens and blues, I saw something. . . a very large bird, I thought, flying very fast—not too, too far away. As I peered intently, I could have sworn I saw legs dangling from the underbelly.

On my way home I saw something very strange.

The bird disappeared into the shadows of the horizon.

Or was it a bird? Was it even there? Had I seen anything at all?

I didn't dwell on what I'd seen. But neither was I able to remove the memory from my mind.

⇜

IN 1984 I WAS, IN MY GROWN-UP JOB as a nature writer, researching an article on *Rangifer tarandus*—the reindeer family. I had already learned whatever I could from books—"Reindeer are Arctic and sub-Arctic deer, the North American species of which is called caribou. They are characterized by the possession of antlers by both sexes, they have large lateral hooves and hairy muzzles, and a curious type of antler with the brow-tine directed downwards. The compact, dense coat is usually clove-brown in color above and white below, with a white tail-patch. . ."—I had read all that kind of thing. And now I wanted to go north to see for myself, to watch the animal in its native habitat, to observe its behavior.

So I made my way to a small Inuit village in far northern Canada called Kuujjuaq. Ever since, it has lived in my mind as a place of great import, a village of wisdom, grace and even magic.

⇜

I STAYED WITH AN INUIT FAMILY, very gentle, quiet and good-humored folks.[1] I learned a great deal about reindeer by watching several species in their natural surroundings at Ungava Bay, and I became aware of Inuit customs, too. I learned about Inuit traditions and Inuit religion. Some of the people's beliefs were steeped in a northern mythology. Much of it seemed pretty strange to

[1] We often call these natives of northern Canada "Eskimos," but they call themselves Inuit, which means simply, "the people."

me—legends of singing fish, whales with horns like unicorns, ghost bears. Most of the traditions had to do with animals.

The Inuit were not at all insulted when I appeared surprised by some of their stories and superstitions. They would often laugh quietly among themselves. "Yes," my hostess once said. "I have never seen the ghost bear, and I never expect to see him either!" But the Inuit were adamant on the subject of reindeer. They believed, beyond any doubt, that reindeer could fly.

The fervor with which my hosts talked of flying reindeer made an impression on me. This wasn't a singing fish, this was something else. They just wouldn't hear a discouraging word on the subject. "The reindeer fly," my host once told me. "It is simple. It is like the moon. Like fire. It is hard to understand, but it just *is*."

Their passion on this single and singular assertion led me to wonder.

WONDER, YES, but certainly not believe. I kept expressing doubt, mildly and politely, but emphatically. They would just shake their heads and say, "Of course it is true." Sometimes they would smile, but they weren't laughing with me on this one. They were laughing *at* me.

The Inuit seem to regard the one we call "Santa Claus" not only as a miracle worker but also as a friend and neighbor.

On a cold, gray day in November, my host and hostess took me down to the village's "museum," which was actually just a shack, way out at the end of a winding, lonely, little-used dirt road. I brought my camera, and I have since congratulated myself for remembering it.

Inside the shack there were all these old—I guess you'd call them scrapbooks. They lay scattered and uncatalogued on shelves of unpainted wood. The room was lit only by our lantern; it was not a particularly pleasant place, that museum. But there were those books that my friends insisted I see. I took several of them to the dusty wood table in the center of the museum's single room. I sat down on a rickety wooden chair.

The pages of the first book were made of leather. Between these heavy leaves were etchings on birch bark, scraps of very old writings, knife drawings—all kinds of things. The illustrations were of animals that were supposed to be walking, talking and, yes, flying. Many of these animals were reindeer. These weren't exactly funny sketches— they certainly weren't intended to be— but if they had been, you might have said they had been drawn by an ancient, Inuit Dr. Seuss.

I asked my host if the illustrations existed simply because Inuit believed reindeer had a sacred aspect. Maybe the ancient artists were

likening reindeer to angels? My host insisted this was not the case. "They fly," was all he said.

There was one item... I'd call it a drawing. It was an etching on leather, done with the point of a knife. It obviously showed a deer pulling a sled, seen in front of a full moon. I asked the Inuit if this was supposed to be Santa Claus. "Who is Sand in Claws?" my hostess asked. I soon discovered that Inuit ideas of who delivers the gifts on December 25th are quite different from ours. The man we know as Saint Nicholas does indeed have a place among the Inuit, but he is no red-suited, ho-ho-ho ball of fun to them. He's an Inuit saint, a man of great seriousness and firm intent. They claim to know him as an ancestor. "He came this way one thousand years ago," said my host. "He lived to the east, some five hundred miles. But only for a very short time. And then he went north. He left behind many small deer."

As we left the museum, my Inuit friends could tell that I still didn't accept the idea of flying deer. I was trying to be agreeable, but they could tell.

In the north, a reindeer represents a noble spirit as well as a source of food and even a means of transport.

THEY DISCUSSED their next step at a community council to which I was not invited. Then, just before I was to leave Kuujjuaq, I was escorted by a party of Inuit from the village to a riverbank not far from town. The north-flowing Caniapiscau River enters Ungava Bay just above Kuujjuaq, and that's where we went, to the mouth of the Caniapiscau, where the big stream flattens and grows wide. The Inuit elders—the tribal leaders—obviously had decided that this field trip was an acceptable thing to do. And so, while I sensed some slight hesitancy about unveiling whatever secret was going to be unveiled, our little party made its way through the trees to the river.

When we arrived at the Caniapiscau, we pushed aside the brush, and there before us, as if made to order, was a mammoth deer. He weighed, I would say, about six or perhaps even seven hundred pounds. He was very big for a reindeer. He was one of the extensive St. George's herd, the herd I had traveled to Kuujjuaq to learn about.

He was browsing at the edge of the forest. As I say, you come across reindeer everywhere up there—the St. George's herd comprises 300,000 deer, spread all over northeastern Canada. So it was nothing unusual to find this big fellow munching lichen by the river. I had been watching him and his brethren deer move alone or in groups for nearly a month, and I felt I had come to understand them. I felt, in my arrogance, that I knew just about everything there was to know about them.

And then...

And then it happened. Suddenly this enormous buck stopped, turned, took a short run and—after a soft grunt and a forceful liftoff—he soared across the water. It was astonishing: two hundred yards in a single bound! He was in the air forever, it seemed.

He was flying.

I gasped, then shivered. I was too stunned to snap even one picture.

The Inuit said that this was nothing compared with what "the little ones" could do. "The little ones that live farther north," one man said. "Those are the *real* fliers."

EVER SINCE MY EXPERIENCE in the far north I have spent whatever free time I have had investigating this flying-deer phenomenon, and how it applies to Santa Claus's annual Mission. I had gone to Kuujjuaq to investigate the biology and physi-

THE LEATHER ETCHING

ology that govern the earthbound lives of reindeer. I came away determined to unravel a far greater mystery.

I have, by now, read dozens of books—both old and new—on reindeer and caribou: books of natural history and books of pure mythology. I have found a clue here and a clue there, a possible source here and another there—I've even found an old photo-

graph of Inuit looking skyward, at what seem to be flying deer. I have learned of several people who have first- or second-hand information concerning Santa Claus and his tremendous undertaking. It turns out there is a small network of

When poring over photographs in one collection of Arctic artifacts, I was astonished to find this image— undated, unsigned but wholly real.

people around the world that helps the great elf, and I have been fortunate in gaining the confidence of this network.

I promised that I would never try to exploit or in any way intrude upon Santa Claus and his Christmas Mission. But, I said, I needed to understand some things. And I added that I

was sure others wanted to understand as well. An interesting discovery: As I reached deeper into this marvelous story, I learned that although Santa Claus feels strongly that he and his elves must live and toil in isolation, he is not at all reluctant to have us know certain facts about his Mission. In fact, he seems to *want* us to know. In 1986 he told Will Steger— the Minnesota adventurer who is the only person alive to have ventured into Claus's North Pole camp—that he is happy to divulge how he does what he does. "Because," he told Steger, "then maybe people will understand *why* I do it."

I HOPED to come to some better understanding of this "why." But to get there, I realized I needed to figure out the "what" and the "how"—What did Santa Claus do each year, and how did he do it? What I needed to know about was this: There was once an Inuit somewhere in Canada—a hunter who lived long, long ago. On a midnight, moonlight hunt, something strange and wonderful had happened in the sky, and he had seen it. He had been moved by it, and he had set it down in an old leather book.

What was it? What had he seen?

What did it mean? Did it have anything to do with that nonbird "bird" I had seen, years before, beyond the far fields and forests of a New England landscape?

You see, I already knew with absolute certainty, deep in my soul, that there was an ancient Inuit who had seen, one December night long ago, a sleigh being pulled by deer and silhouetted against the moon. Fascinated by this vision, he had scratched out a picture with his knife on a piece of leather. This had been saved in a dark little shack on the outskirts of a village named Kuujjuaq. In an old, tattered scrapbook sits a hunter's picture of Santa Claus and a flying reindeer. It is a wondrous thing.

Two items in the museum intrigued me, so I photographed them. In the upper righthand corner of the birch painting, reindeer can be seen taking flight. The leather etching speaks for itself. But what tale does it tell?

The Echo of Hooves

Searching for Yesteryear's Deer

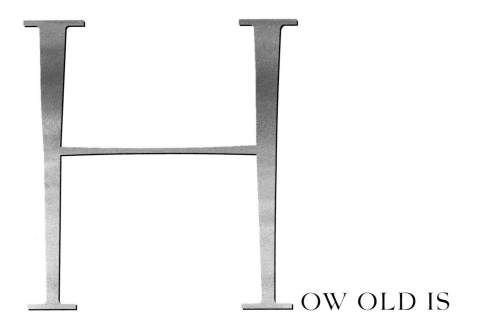

OW OLD IS

the jolly old man? Unless he chooses to tell us—

and it is exceedingly unlikely that he will, for he is

a lovely but reticent man—we will never know. That

is to say, we'll never know how old he is in the way that

we count the years. Surely he is immortal in a spiritual sense.

A ND SURELY HE IS LONG-LIVED in *any* sense because we do know that he has been on the job for nearly two thousand years. There are records of children in northern Africa getting mysterious presents as long ago as that. There are stories of strange midwinter visitations made to Native Americans that long ago. There are aboriginal traditions in Australia that speak of a flying man from the north. There are reports of a curious Arctic city of elves that date that far back. There is even firm support for the claim of those Inuit of Kuujjuaq: Yes, indeed, Santa Claus did pass through their land a thousand years ago. He and his community settled for a short while just to the east, and then—exactly as the Inuit said—they uprooted themselves and went north.

"If you look at the evidence—and I mean *evidence*, not legend—then you arrive at a few pieces of certain knowledge," says Philip N. Cronenwett. "Piece Number One: Santa Claus opened shop two millennia ago, give or take a decade. Piece Number Two: He has been in business every year since, although some years, it is clear, were difficult for him—very hard indeed for him to deliver during those years. Piece Number Three: He has modified his approach, he has gotten better at what he does. Piece Number Four, and this is a tangent to Piece Number Three: He has had to change his location. He did not start all this activity at the North Pole. That's something I find fascinating."

Who is Philip N. Cronenwett, and how does he know these things with such certainty? He is the director of Special Collections at Dartmouth College's Baker

"By reading histories, we can trace the origins of Santa's nation far beyond its establishment at the North Pole."

– PHILIP N. CRONENWETT, *librarian of Arctic studies and authority on northern civilizations*

Library in New Hampshire. Baker's is, perhaps, the finest collection of Arctic artifact and literature in the country. Cronenwett's office is just off the dark, oiled-wood Treasure Room, where the library's most valuable books are kept under lock and key. Cronenwett has read those books, all of them. He has put together the pieces.

"Santa Claus is two things indisputably—he is an elf, and he is a good man," says Cronenwett as he leans back in his chair. "I have never been able to learn where he was born, but I do know that his. . . his 'village' was originally situated in south-central Greenland. Makes sense, when you think about it, that he used to live somewhere else. I mean, why would anyone *choose* to live at the North Pole?"

To support his theories, Cronenwett can cite chapter and verse from great antiquated volumes. "We have writings from eleventh century Iceland," he says, not a little proudly. "We have books depicting cave art from eleventh century Canada—or, rather, the region we now call Canada."

Cronenwett sketches a chronology of dramatic events: A vast community of elves, led by the one who would come to be known as Saint Nicholas or, more commonly, Santa Claus, was established in Greenland untold centuries ago. It was quite near what is now a small town known as Holsteinborg, and the citizens of Holsteinborg have found many relics from Claus's first settlement.

This, of course, fits well with established histories of elfin communities, none of which suggest elves emigrated south from the Pole. In fact, elves probably originated in Iceland, then quite quickly spread to Greenland, Ireland and the northern reaches of the European conti-

ELVES   GNOMES   LOVELINGS   LIGHT-FAIRIES

DWARVES   ANGELS   MOUNTAIN SPIRITS

nent. If you are looking for an elfin Eden—a place of origin for little people—you'd do well to look at the Icelandic town of Hafnarfjördur. Relics found there indicate a veritable beehive of "hidden worlds." On the outskirts of town, angelic beings are said to dwell on the Hamarinn Cliff and all up and down Mount Asfjall. In town, some twenty different types of elf live (or have lived in past generations). In the western sector, the conical houses of elves proliferate, and in the Tjarnargata district there is a dense community of dwarves. "We have known for a long time of another society coexistent with our human one, a community concealed from most people with its dwellings in many parts of town and in the lava and cliffs that surround it," says Ingvar Viktorsson, mayor of Hafnarfjördur. "We are convinced that the elves, hidden people and other beings living there are favorably disposed towards us and are as fond of our town as we are."

A catalog of hidden beings: In Iceland, all manner of them abound—animal and spiritual.

The variety and number of souls throughout Hafnarfjördur suggest that here is where it might have started for all the world's small ones—and that here, indeed, is where Santa Claus's forebears probably once dwelled. In the Town Hall there are records of who is suspected of living where, and in an afternoon's visit you can put together an extraordinary census for Hafnarfjördur:

⌐ Elves (in Icelandic, *alfar*), some twenty types;

⌐ Gnomes (*jarodvergar*), related to elves but no more than seven inches tall, four types;

⌐ Lovelings (*ljuflingar*), the size of ten-year-old children, usually live behind hedgerows and in woodlands, at least two types;

⌐ Light-fairies (*ljosalfar*), resembling angels but tinier, dwelling near lakes, one type;

⌐ Dwarves (*dvergar*), squat creatures the size of three-year-old humans, six types including the temperamental beings and the sweet-natured ones;

☞ Angels (*englar*), as many as a dozen types, to the very highest illuminations;

☞ Mountain Spirits (*tivar*), one type—but this one, living on Asfjall, is said by those who've seen it to be the most radiant anywhere in the world.

Clearly, Hafnarfjördur has long been a fertile, nurturing place for what some call "the wee people." A last point to be made, before returning to the community led by Santa Claus, is this: The citizens of Hafnarfjördur, hidden and nonhidden, have longstanding traditions of good community relations, serenity, generosity and industriousness. These are, of course, qualities often associated with Santa Claus generally, and specifically with The Christmas Mission.

WE DON'T KNOW WHEN the Claus clan emigrated from Iceland to Greenland, but we do know that Santa Claus's "village" in Greenland was a thriving town, and that its main concentration was manufacturing. For nearly a thousand years, from the earliest period A.D. until the turn of the first millennium, the centerpiece of this society was its annual Mission, a fantastic one-night global voyage, the intent of which was, from the first, to bring cheer to the world's least fortunate. "We know of this intent from the testimony Will Steger brought back from the North Pole in 1986," says Cronenwett. "What an extraordinary thing— a first-hand interview with Claus. A meeting with the elves! A tour of the village. I've always been deeply envious."

Steger tells us—because Santa Claus told *him*— that near the end of the first millennium the elves fled Greenland.

History tells us why.

In the 10th century, human beings—Inuit, Sami,

Elves' Exodus

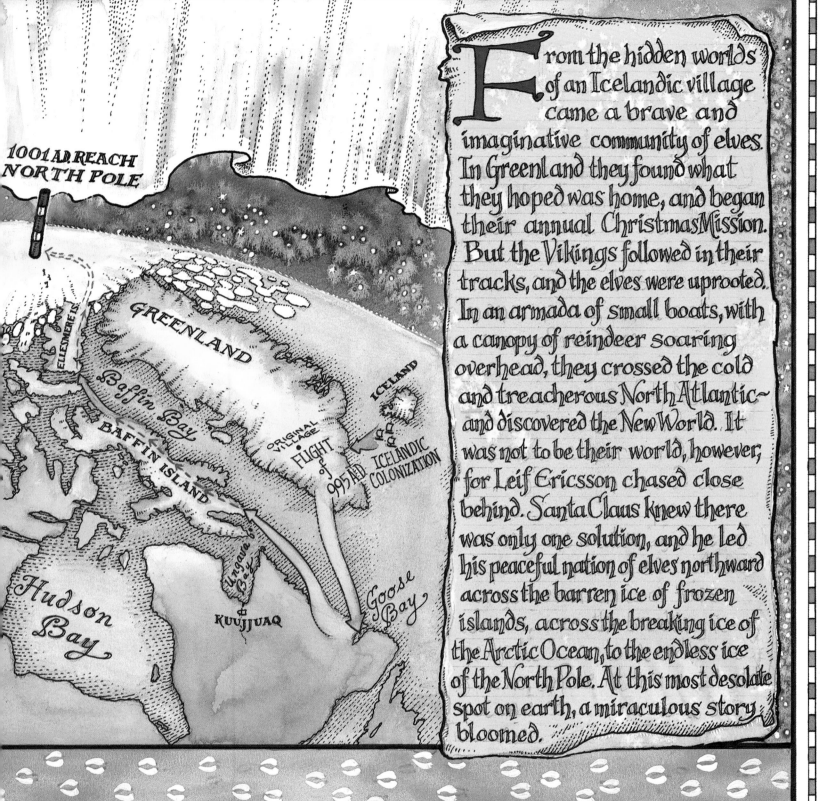

1001 A.D. REACH NORTH POLE

GREENLAND

ELLESMERE IS.

Baffin Bay

BAFFIN ISLAND

Hudson Bay

Ungava Bay

KUUJJUAQ

Goose Bay

ICELAND

ORIGINAL VILLAGE

FLIGHT of 995 A.D.

ICELANDIC COLONIZATION

From the hidden worlds of an Icelandic village came a brave and imaginative community of elves. In Greenland they found what they hoped was home, and began their annual Christmas Mission. But the Vikings followed in their tracks, and the elves were uprooted. In an armada of small boats, with a canopy of reindeer soaring overhead, they crossed the cold and treacherous North Atlantic— and discovered the New World. It was not to be their world, however, for Leif Ericsson chased close behind. Santa Claus knew there was only one solution, and he led his peaceful nation of elves northward across the barren ice of frozen islands, across the breaking ice of the Arctic Ocean, to the endless ice of the North Pole. At this most desolate spot on earth, a miraculous story bloomed.

Lapp—started to drift onto Greenland from Iceland, Labrador and elsewhere. Whether their presence was of any concern to Claus's elf community is unclear, but it seems Santa Claus has always been less wary of northern-folk than of Europeans, for whatever reasons.

In the year 982 a Viking chieftain in Iceland named Eric the Red was convicted of certain crimes, and was sent into exile for three years. His banishment took him to

Word of this seeped inland, and Santa Claus decided that his own small nation had to be moved. Elves can live five thousand years, but only if they are left unharmed. They are so small and so docile by nature that they present no match for humans.

Claus acted quickly and forcefully when he learned of a European presence on the island, says Cronenwett. He moves from his office into the Treasure Room where, from

In European art, flying animals are prevalent. The Italian woodcut, circa 1500, shows a dragon pulling a sleigh, while the 19th century Norwegian print depicts men stunned by deer.

Greenland. On returning to his homeland, he began to sing the praises of this other, larger isle. He urged colonization, and in the spring of 986, twenty-five ships headed across the Greenland Sea laden with fowl, farm animals and 750 Icelanders. The passage was treacherous, and only fourteen ships survived. But a foothold had been gained, and in the next few years thousands of Icelanders joined their Norse kinfolk in the *Osterbygd*, or "eastern settlement."

a glass case, he takes two mammoth volumes bound in leather—*Journals of the Osterbygd.* "Look here," he says as he leafs through the ancient pages. "You can't read the words because they're in Old Icelandic, but in translation this page recounts, 'Activity to the west... Eskimo? Elves?... Night movement sighted by scouting parties?' And over here..." He turns several more pages. "This says, in translation, that the Vikings found an intact, absolutely abandoned city of five miles square, a city that would have housed people less than half their own size. You see? I think what this means is, Eric's men found Santa's first village! But they were too late. The whole Claus nation was able to beat it out of there before the Vikings swooped down. It's one of the great reconnaissances in history."

Einar Gustavsson, a native of the northern Iceland village of Siglufjördur and an expert translator of Old

entire village simply pulled up stakes—*poof!*—and fled westward. Santa Claus was then, as he is today, the most knowledgeable navigator on earth. It's clear that he plotted every latitude and longitude from the air centuries before any Europeans got around to mapping the face of the earth—that amazing route map they found in Norway in 1654 proves it. Therefore, he knew exactly where he was going. His people made landfall in what is now Labrador

Two runners-up: Leif Ericsson (left) thought he was the first European in the New World when he came ashore at Baffin Island in 1001, and Christopher Columbus (below) thought he was first when he reached the Bahamas in 1492.

Icelandic, has read the ancient texts and has worked hard to visualize this first escape of Santa Claus. In relating the tale, he propounds an extraordinary thesis, one that instantly alters what we know of western history. "They traveled overland by dogsled, then oversea by boats," says Gustavsson during an interview in Reykjavik, the capital of Iceland. "This is not to mention *overhead*, via scores of provision-packed sleds pulled by the flying reindeer. The

in Canada, then went south and set up an elfin city in what is now called Goose Bay. It's interesting that this was the only time Santa Claus ever headed south—he's certainly a north-bearing man. But what I find *much* more interesting is this: If you consider Santa Claus a European, as we Icelanders do, then you must consider him—not Leif Ericsson and certainly not Christopher Columbus—to be the very first from the Old World to discover the New!"

LEIF WOULD NOT BE FAR BEHIND. Eric the Red's son became, in the year 1000, the first Viking to view the mainland of North America. And to be viewed in turn. From the harbor where his commune was taking root, Santa Claus saw Ericsson's ships. He knew what he had to do.

"Leaving Labrador for the Arctic was the only option available," says Cronenwett. "He must have known the only place in the whole world where he would be left alone was on the polar ice cap. And he knew that his elves were the only beings on the planet who could survive where there was no place to grow food—no ground, no soil, nothing. How? The flying deer would allow them to establish an operation that imported food! My guess is that Santa knew that whatever provisions they needed in those difficult early years could be scavenged at night throughout Europe, Asia and North America by reindeer-riding elves, who would then fly back to the Pole. In a way, they were the original homeless people of the northern world. Until they got the village up and running, they basically lived on scraps."

The exodus of elves to the North Pole was a difficult one, over the windswept hills of Baffin and Ellesmere Islands, and finally to the Arctic cap. There, in the late spring of 1001, the elves saw the great ice of the far northern Atlantic start to break up behind them, giving way to open, frigid, impassable water. Fatal water. They looked back from their new, eternally floating homeland on the ice and knew that they had severed ties forever with all earthly continents.

Except... They hadn't. For decades they came each night for food. And, of course, once a year, every year, they—or at

least *he*—returned to carry out the extraordinary Mission that was theirs and theirs alone. The assignment—given to them by God knows who—was to provide Christmas each 24th and 25th of December. Through struggle and courage they found the one perfect place in the wide world from which to do it.

CERTAINLY, Claus could not have made good his flight were it not for a number of factors peculiar to him and his people. First, they're very small.[2] And elfin communities are known to be as stealthy as any the world has ever produced—stealthier by far than societies of gnomes or dwarves. Claus's people, in particular, seem blessed with an uncanny ability to travel largely undetected (which is not to say unseen) and to leave few tracks. "Now you glimpse 'em, now you don't," says Oran Young, a colleague and good friend of Cronenwett's at Dartmouth and head of the college's Institute of Arctic Studies. "All northernfolk know they're up there. There's mountains and mountains of circumstantial evidence, and tons of lore that *borders* on fact. But if you say to the Inuit or the Sami, 'Prove it!' not many of them can. They say, 'Well, I saw this,' or 'I saw that,' but not a lot of them will say, 'Look at this here elf's cap!' Claus and his colleagues are superb at covering their footprints. The only reason we can speak of them with any certainty is the cumulative record built over two millennia, and bits of first-hand evidence like Steger's."

The elves' size is advantageous in other ways as well. They have a unique metabolism, and need precious little food to generate enormous amounts of energy; Santa

"Elves are tiny, their reindeer are tiny, their city is tiny. This is why they're so seldom seen."

– ORAN YOUNG,
*Arctic Institute
director and hidden-
world historian*

[2] Each elf is between two and three feet tall; Santa himself is only an inch or two taller than the rest.

ALASKA MOOSE

Alecs alecs
WORLD'S LARGEST DEER
SHOULDER HEIGHT ~ UP TO 7½'
WEIGHT ~ UP TO 1800 LBS.
7"

AMERICAN ELK

Cervus elaphus americanus
SHOULDER HEIGHT ~ UP TO 5'
WEIGHT ~ UP TO 800 LBS.
4½"

LAPLAND REINDEER

Rangifer tarandus tarandus
SHOULDER HEIGHT ~ UP TO 4'
WEIGHT ~ UP TO 400 LBS.
5"

WHITE ~ TAILED DEER

Odocoileus virginianus
SHOULDER HEIGHT ~ UP TO 3¾'
WEIGHT ~ UP TO 350 LBS.
4"

PEARY CARIBOU

Rangifer tarandus pearyi
SANTA'S REINDEER
SHOULDER HEIGHT ~ 3'+
WEIGHT ~ UP TO 200 LBS.
3"

Claus certainly factored this in when he made the hard choice to head for the barren, foodless North Pole. Still, they eventually would have starved without the big factor. We're refering to flight, of course.

Flight is the salient point, the essential ingredient. Santa Claus's was the first of all the world's communities to be gifted with the ability to fly. Were it not for their tiny reindeer, they couldn't have reached the Pole, they couldn't have thrived at the Pole. Were it not for the reindeer, all that we know about Santa Claus would be contained in weathered Norse history books. Were it not for the reindeer, the elf nation that brings us Christmas might have ended long ago in Greenland.

But it did not—because of Santa Claus, because of his people's courage. And because of the reindeer.

⁓

NOT JUST ANY REINDEER. The deer in question is a certain species, *Rangifer tarandus pearyi*—the Peary caribou. These are "the little ones" spoken of by the Inuit of Kuujjuaq.[3]

First, we must understand that caribou and reindeer are essentially the same animal. The Old World reindeer is the same as the New World caribou, genetically speaking. There are woodland and barren-ground reindeer, and there are several subspecies of each. The biggest woodland animals stand about as high as a man's shoulder and

"There is reindeer cave art in Australia, in Africa, in South America. You tell me how it got there!"

– CARLTON PLUMMER,
art professor emeritus and collector of cave paintings

weigh 600 pounds or more; the smallest barren-ground reindeer look like big dogs with horns and weigh only about 150 pounds. Most reindeer have coats that are brown on top and white on the underbelly, but one particular subspecies is *snow-white* in color. These are the smallest, most northern, most purely white reindeer on the face of the earth. And while other reindeer can fly, it is these that fly best, farthest, fastest.

How old is the Peary? That's impossible to say. The first deer of any kind appeared about ten million years ago in the Pliocene Epoch, but whether Peary were among the early species is uncertain. "Mankind has been on the earth for only several thousand years," says Bil Gilbert, the esteemed natural history writer. "We know the Peary is much older than man. More we cannot say. But he's a feisty animal, compact, hard to see and hard to hunt—not least because he can just take off and fly away. So I would suspect he's probably been around and thriving for a good long while."

Gilbert, relaxing by the stream that passes behind his ranch in Fairfield, Pennsylvania, continues: "The Peary is a fine, peaceful animal—a credit to the planet. Humankind, throughout our own brief history, has always related positively to the Peary in particular, and to all reindeer generally. You can tell from all the cave art." Indeed, in his definitive book *Prehistoric Cave Paintings*, Max Raphael writes of drawings made many centuries ago in Les Combarelles, France: "The horses are repeatedly represented as hostile to the bison and bulls; the reindeer as friendly to mammoths. . . . Everywhere the reindeer live a bright cheerful idyll, just as the bison live a stormy drama." The images

[3] Peary caribou have been "the deer in question" for two thousand years, but of course they were not called Peary caribou until 1909, when American adventurer Robert Peary became the first man to travel overland to the North Pole and, subsequently, got a subspecies of deer named after him in tribute.

in Raphael's book show buoyant reindeer that look to be dancing or, perhaps, flying.

"Sure, there's all sorts of iconography indicating reindeer flight," says Carlton Plummer, professor emeritus at the University of Massachusetts at Lowell. Plummer is a painter himself, and an expert on primitive art. "But what you have to do is separate representations of myth from realistic interpretations. Were those ancient people in France drawing what they truly saw, or just what they *believed*? Were they journalists or myth-mongers?" He pauses, then adds quietly, "Of course, there have been many, many flying-reindeer finds in the Southern Hemisphere too, and that's the rub. The reindeer is an Arctic animal—strictly Northern Hemisphere—so how would people down there have known of it back in ancient times? I mean, of course, unless they *saw* one. And how could they have seen one, unless. . . .Well, *unless one had flown over!*"

A reindeer on a rock wall in southwestern France, painted by the Lascaux artists sometime between 12,000 and 30,000 years ago, clearly shows the animal in an attitude of liftoff.

LET US BE CONSERVATIVE and say that, on the evidence of cave paintings, man has been thinking about flying reindeer for at least 5,000 years. That's fine, because our interest is in the Santa Claus story, and that is a story which, it appears, extends back only 2,000 years. So by the time Claus and his

people started making their efforts known to the rest of the planet, reindeer flight was a commonly regarded phenomenon.

And then, suddenly, in the earliest years A.D., gifts started falling from the sky.

"It's almost a footnote to history," says Forrest Church, pastor of All Souls Church in New York City and author of *Everyday Miracles* and several other books about religion. "This is the mystery-gifts phenomenon that occurred in Africa and southwestern Asia back then. Those were the only cultures on Earth with reliable chroniclers, and when you read their reports about these strange visitations, you develop an odd impression—that this was just an incidental thing to these writers, a very small thing."

He picks up a piece of paper from his cluttered desk. "Here, I'll quote from one. This one was found somewhere in Palestine, and my translation is pretty rough, but it reads as follows: 'And in a strange situation, it appears the poorest of the poor were visited Tuesday last, and were given bread and wine. Of the same night, several children of our settlement were visited as well, and given trinkets.' It goes on, but not much longer. It wasn't news, really, it was just a curiosity—this gift-giving. Why wasn't it a bigger deal? Well, you see, it was a time of great turmoil in the civilized world, and obviously there were more pressing things to talk about than these unconfirmed stories about children and peasants being given tokens by some wandering stranger."

Church pauses. "And also," he says, being playful, as though offering a riddle. "Think about it—there's another reason why it wasn't big news. *No one could have known that it was global.*"

Church continues with a smile, enjoying the moment: "You see, a kid in Rome wakes up on December 25th and finds a gift, and the same thing happens in Athens on the same day. But who could've put two and two together? It was local news, minor neighborhood gossip. There was no quick communication between settlements, between towns, between regions. It is only with hundreds of years of hindsight, and ten thousand excavations, that we can see what was going on. We add this report here to that one from over there, and soon we see the truth—on the same night, in places all over the world, charity was being offered. Why? We don't know. We've never known. But we do know one thing. We can tell from the local histories that it happened once and only once each year. Year after year after year. It was an annual signal to us—an anniversary, a reminder.

"Of what? Well, to be charitable, maybe. To think about the least fortunate. To be generous. To live each day as if you would deserve such a reward as this. I can't say for sure, though I wish I could."

BACK IN THOSE EARLY YEARS of Santa Claus's visits, not only was the elf's reindeer not called the Peary but the elf wasn't called Santa Claus. "He answers to that now," says Will Steger, the famous adventurer from Ely, who actually asked Claus

> "Saint Nicholas was an exemplary human being. Santa Claus is an exemplary elf. What's the problem?"
>
> – FORREST CHURCH, *minister, theologian, historian*

about this. "All the kids of the world call him Santa, so it's fine with him. But his elves know him as something else. It has many syllables, and it really sings—*La-la-fla-yah*-something. I tried to pronounce it, and simply could not do it. That was strange. I just couldn't make the words come out of my mouth."

When the name-change occurred is hard to pinpoint, but it had to have happened in the 4th century A.D. or later. "Yes, absolutely, he worked for at least three hundred years under his real name, whatever it is," says Church, who is equal parts scholar and Unitarian minister. "You could say 'Santa Claus' is his Christian name, because he got it when people started confusing him with a famous and very popular Christian saint—a man, not an elf. The confusion was natural because the North Pole elf and the very human man, Saint Nicholas, were both famous, principally, for their charity and gift-giving. The confusion started sometime in the Middle Ages, and slowly the two figures grew into one—at least in the mind of the world's children."

WHO WAS THIS SAINT Nicholas?
He was a man born late in the 3rd century in Patara, which used to be a city in what is now Turkey. He was a devout and serious child, and as a boy he made a pilgrimage to Palestine, seeking knowledge. He entered a monastery and became a priest when he was only nineteen years old. He was known as a loving minister. There is a tempera painting on wood panel (facing page) done many years after his death by Carlo Crivelli that shows a stern Saint Nicholas. But look closely at the forehead, at the

eyes: There is kindness there, for those who are good.

Nicholas became Bishop of Myra in Lycia on the coast of what was then Asia Minor. There is a legend that he was imprisoned during Diocletian's persecution, then released under Constantine the Great—but much about this man is uncertain. He may never have been imprisoned, may never have needed release.

There is one tale, however, that makes its way to our time having been told over and over again. It takes on the air of truth because so many believe it. It is this:

Nicholas came to know a poor man with a large family. The man had three daughters, each of them personable, intelligent and altogether companionable. But no man would marry any of the daughters because the father could not provide a dowry. The father grew saddened, the daughters despondent. Then, one December night, Nicholas passed by the family's house. He threw three bags of money through an open window. (Who does *that* sound

A serious Nicholas is depicted in this painting, executed by Crivelli in 1472 and now on display at the Cleveland Museum of Art.

like?) Each of the girls now had a dowry, each of them married, and the legend of Saint Nicholas as a secret gift-giver was born.

But not only as a gift giver.

As "One who helps the poor."

As "One who understands."

As one who sees bright futures for the young, inspiring them to always be at their best.

After his death, Nicholas was credited with having performed many miracles. He was beatified, and came to be considered the patron saint of sailors, travelers, bakers, scholars, merchants, of all of Russia—but most importantly, of children. He became famous throughout the world, and by the Middle Ages traditions were springing up that were associated with him.

His feast day was celebrated on December 6th. In many European countries this became a day of celebration and gift-giving.

IT'S EASY TO SEE how the confusion started, what with the saint having an annual day in his honor—during which gifts were exchanged—and the elf making his surreptitious visits in the same season. From the year 1000 until approximately 1500, the images blurred further, with the saint getting more and more credit for the elf's work, with the elf taking on the saint's name in country after country, with the saint taking on elfin characteristics in certain cultures, with the elf starting to look more and more like a man.

As for the name, it came by way of Holland. Of all the places where Saint Nicholas was popular, he was most beloved in the Scandinavian countries and in the Netherlands. The Dutch for "Saint Nicholas" is *Sinterklass*, and when this term made its way to the English-speaking world, "Santa Claus" was born. Because of various pictures of the human saint that were available, the winter visitor from the North Pole acquired a physical image that would not be corrected until the 1800s. For centuries, most people thought "Claus" was a tall man who wore bishop's robes and rode a white horse. Children throughout Europe would leave carrots and hay for the horse on the special eve, and must have wondered why only the carrots—a vegetable that Peary

On one level, it seems odd that the elf was confused with a man at least twice his size.

caribou adore—were gone the next morn.

Not all countries called the mysterious visitor Santa Claus or even Saint Nicholas. In Germany he was *Knecht Ruprecht*, or Servant Rupert. In Italy he—or, rather, *she*— was *Le Befana*, a kindly old witch. In England he was Father Christmas, and on this point—if few others—France agreed with England, calling him *Père Noel*.

Why all the variation? Because no one was sure. No one could pin him down precisely. Those who came closest were those who were geographically and spiritually nearest to him: the Scandinavians. Swedish children, it was said, received gifts from the elf *Jultomten*, and Danes and Norwegians were visited by an elf they called *Julenissen*. "We know they found evidence of Santa's elves—that map, for instance—since they lived way up there near the Pole," says Young of the Institute of Arctic Studies. "I've always figured that's why their version of Santa Claus is closest to the real thing."

It was in the early 1800s that Americans started to know the real thing better. The writer Washington Irving played a large part in this. He spent much of the first decade of the century researching traditions concerning the Christmas holiday and its famous present-bearer. In 1809 Irving published the fruits of his labor. To give an idea of the portrait he painted, there is this, concerning a visit by the elf to New York state: "And lo, the good Saint Nicholas came riding over the tops of the trees, in that self-same wagon wherein he brings his yearly presents to children, and he descended hard by where the heroes of Communipaw had made their late repast. And he lit his pipe by the fire, and sat himself down and smoked; and as he smoked the smoke from his pipe ascended into the air and spread like a cloud overhead. . . . And when Saint Nicholas had smoked his pipe, he twisted it in his hat-band, and laying his finger beside his nose, gave the astonished Van Kortlandt a very significant look, then mounting his wagon he returned over the tree-tops and disappeared." And later: "Thus, having quietly settled themselves down, and provided for their own comfort, they bethought themselves of testifying their gratitude to the great and good Saint Nicholas. . . . At this early period was

instituted that pious ceremony, still religiously observed in all our ancient families of the right breed, of hanging up a stocking in the chimney on Saint Nicholas eve; which stocking is always found in the morning miraculously filled; for the good Saint Nicholas has ever been a great giver of gifts, particularly to children."

With these words America's first great man of letters was codifying a vision of the December visitor: the most accurate description of Claus yet presented anywhere in the world. Substitute "sleigh" for "wagon"—and what historian might not suffer a trivial mistake like that?—and it becomes evident that Irving's was a remarkable achievement.

"Irving was a brilliant man," says Regina Barreca, professor of English at the University of Connecticut and an expert on British and American literature. "Careful, thoughtful, thorough. He was just as great a biographer as he was a writer of fiction. When he turned to biography, he didn't choose to write about just anyone. He liked to deal with the true

In the 19th century, Nast's illustrations (top) and the word portraits of Irving (seated) gave us an accurate picture of the elf.

giants—the biggest of the big. He gave us masterful portraits of George Washington, of Shakespeare and, of course, of Santa Claus."

What was Irving's source material? "I presume Irving found copies of the Greenland journals, and there were also several Scandinavian histories concerning elves published right about that time," says Dartmouth's Cronenwett. "We have some of them on our shelves, though we certainly didn't have them back then. Irving would have been able to acquire them because he was one of the first American authors to travel extensively in England and Europe. He spent an awful lot of time in London doing research, and these books, which would *not* have made their way to the U.S. until much later, would have been available there."

⤳

IRVING'S VERSION of Santa Claus was confirmed and elaborated on throughout the remainder of the 19th century. There were many reported sightings, of which the 1847 group sighting in Durango, Colorado, is perhaps the most famous. From *The Durango Nugget*, December 26, 1847: "Mike and Janice Larkin were hosting their annual 'Dark Night Dance' at their cabin on the mountain Friday night when a noise was heard and all the guests made for the porch. 'Sounded like dynamite,' Larkin said. 'But who would be blasting at that time of night? So we went to see and, I swear, a flash of light just zoomed up over the far hills, it looked like a star flying by, but closer. It was weird, son, real weird.' Larkin's guests confirmed this account."

There were the visual interpretations of Thomas Nast in several issues of *Harper's Weekly* from 1863 to

"Without the good, honest reporting of Irving, Moore and others, it would be much harder to believe in Santa."

— REGINA BARRECA,
literature professor and Santa Claus scholar

1890. There was Clement Clark Moore's famous 19th century poem "An Account of a Visit from St. Nicholas" that enlarged and embellished the Irving Santa. It is interesting and a bit sad to note that this poem, which begins with the famous line "Twas the night before Christmas," may not have been written by Moore at all, but by a man named Henry Livingston. Moore was credited because, as a renowned scholar, he was believed more capable of insight into Claus's character than was Livingston, a land surveyor by trade.

There were even those strange photographs of unidentified flying objects. Many remain unexplained. Some people think they're spaceships, others insist they are merely photographic illusions. Undeniably, a few of these photos are taunting in the extreme. Look hard at Bill Johnson's famous image taken in far northern New Hampshire, in a tiny village with the cold and lonely name of Stark (population, 350). Yes, sure, it could have been a speck on Johnson's lens as he turned his camera toward the moon late one night in December. Or it could have been a reindeer, flying. Imagine it: He is traveling slowly—slowly enough to forge a distinct image on film, instead of just a blur—as he heads back to the North Pole following a workout. The Stark Image beguiles and bedevils us.

There were these things and others to lead us closer to an understanding of Santa Claus—who he was and what he did.

But, still. . .

No one had yet met him.

No one had gone north to the Pole.

No one had seen the village.

No one knew the secrets behind the miracle.

Johnson remembers:
"The covered bridge at
Stark never looked lovelier
than it did on that night.
The air was frigid and I
was absolutely alone.
Then, suddenly, in
front of the moon—
There it was!"

PART TWO

The North Pole Today

On the Roof of the World

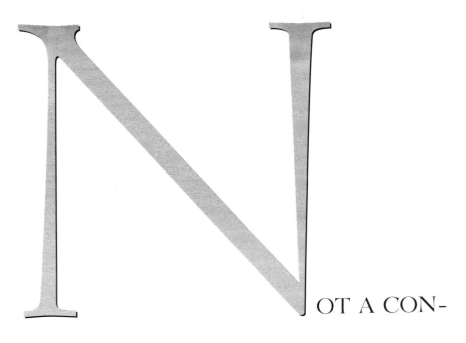

NOT A CONtinent, not a country. It is solid but it is liquid. Nothing grows there and almost no one goes there. It is never in precisely the same place that it was only a moment ago. It is always in flux, shifting and floating. All ice, not a bit of earth beneath it, it is the roof of the world. It is the North Pole.

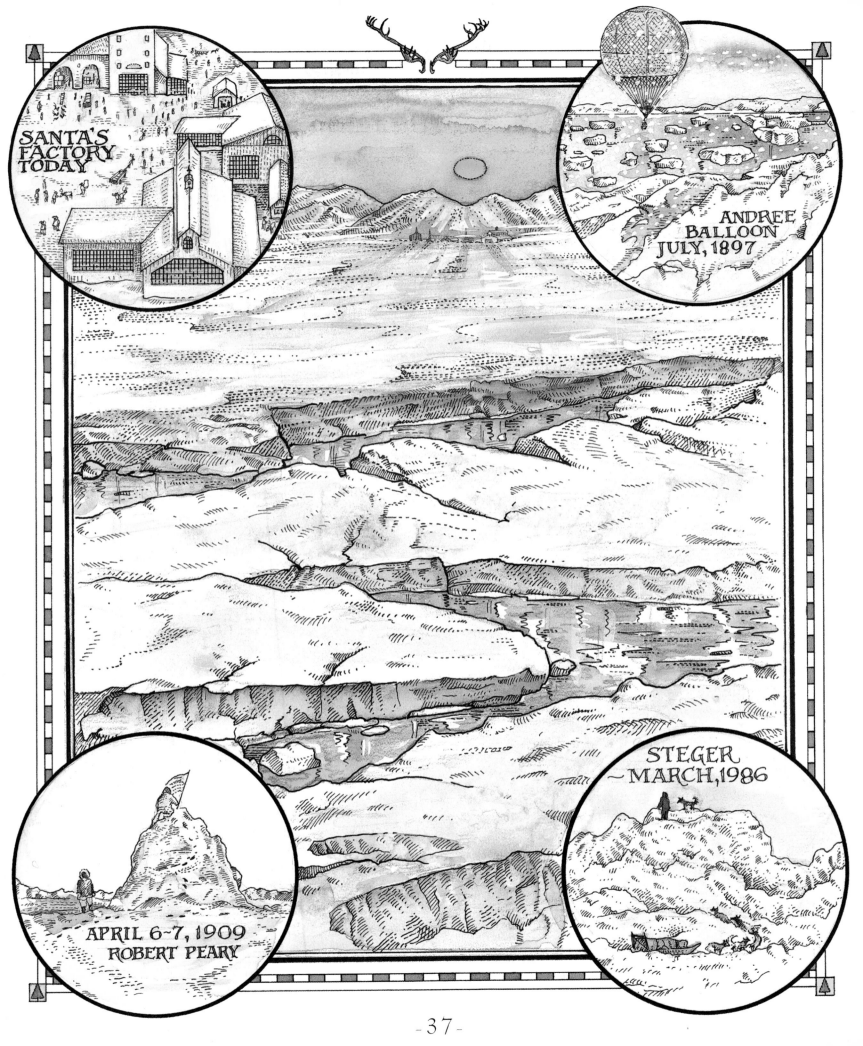

SANTA'S
FACTORY
TODAY

ANDREE
BALLOON
JULY, 1897

STEGER
~ MARCH, 1986

APRIL 6~7, 1909
ROBERT PEARY

"I'VE STUDIED THE NORTH POLE, and I can tell you—it's a very mysterious, almost eerie place," says Dartmouth's Oran Young, who is also vice-president of the International Arctic Science Committee. "There's often fog, and there are these mountains of ice all around. There's absolutely no way Santa Claus and the entire village could be so seldom seen if they were anywhere else on the globe. Every other location is fixed in space and time. Plus, the way the ice floats—swirling and sailing like it does—well, the huge ice ridge that you saw in the west yesterday can be in the north tomorrow, and it can be east the day after that. You start to think your compass is going crazy. It makes Santa's village nearly impossible to locate. It's the only town in the entire world that does not lie at a specific latitude and longitude. It *moves*."

THOSE WHO HAVE SEEN the tiny village have literally stumbled upon it. They have been tourists, glimpsing it through a cloud bank as their airplane flew over the Pole. Or they have been explorers, seeing *something* as they gained the summit of a sheltering ridge of ice. Will Steger is one of the latter, although to say he saw merely "something" is a gross understatemnt. In 1986 Steger went north with his dog team and, near the very top of the planet, realized that he was among the blessed few. "I was driving my team up this ice ridge," he remembers, as he sits by the shore of a lake in back of his rustic cabin in far northern Minnesota. He gazes at the water, and his eyes glisten. "The sled crested, and at that moment the fog blew away. There it was, below us. The whole village. The reindeer. The small sleds being pulled all over the place by deer and elves. The moment I saw it, I was sure it wasn't

"Of course we wondered whether we might see him. But you can't count on much that far north."

– WILL STEGER,
adventurer and the only man to have visited the village

true. I figured I was getting delirious, that the cold and fatigue were finishing me off. I mean, that's an ice world up there. Nothing can live there, right? But I rubbed my eyes, and the village did not vanish. I wondered if I had died, and was maybe in some kind of Arctic heaven."

"Some kind of heaven"—Steger was more right than he realized. He was in an otherworldly kingdom, a place of magic, miracles, nonmortal things. He was in a place humankind had been trying to reach forever.

Some history: The North Pole has always been considered a grail; man has always wanted—needed—to understand the place and those who live there. The ancients believed that there existed a happy region, Boreas, that lay north of the north wind, a place where the sun always shone and the Hyperboreans led a peaceful and productive existence. The Greek Pythias went in search of this happiness in 325 B.C., proceeding northward along Europe's western coast. He made it to Norway, which he called Thule, but he probably didn't reach the Arctic Circle.

In the 9th century a group of Irish monks also quested northward, eventually settling in Iceland; people were getting closer. There were many, many thrusts north throughout the years, most of these by English, Scandinavian and eventually American explorers. But before this century, each effort was stymied by the horrible weather and the various dangers of the polar cap. The ice up there is never smooth; it is thrust up into terrifying ridges with knife-edge peaks. How could anyone travel in such a land?

But the pull of True North was great, and eventually a contest of sorts developed: Who would reach it first? The Englishman David Buchan tried to find the Pole in 1818

Steger's team was only the latest in a very long line that have followed the midnight sun toward True North.

and came nowhere near. Nine years later his countryman William Edward Parry also went north via Spitzbergen, and also came back south in disappointment. In 1871 Charles Hall's third try came to tragedy: He died, and on their attempted return to England half of his crew became stranded on the ice during a storm. They drifted on the frigid sea for six months before being rescued by a whaling boat.

In 1875 British naval officer George Nares failed. In 1882 the U.S. Navy's Lt. George Washington De Long also failed. In 1884 American Brig. Gen. Adolphus Washington Greely led an expedition up the length of Ellesmere Island, and his junior officer, Lt. Lockwood, established a new Farthest North point. But Greely, too, ultimately failed, and six of his twenty-four men died.

IN THE LAST DECADE of the last century, the zeal for getting to the Pole (and to insights about Santa Claus) became feverish. In 1897, a charismatic Scandinavian named Salomon Andree—scientist, athlete, airman—electrified the world and shocked the competition: He would try to reach the Pole in a balloon. The earth's citizens held their breath as Andree and two comrades made their way to the northern coast of Spitzbergen and, on a windy July 11th, lifted off dramatically. "The balloon is now traveling straight to the north; it goes along swiftly," wrote Alexis Machuron, a member of the base party who was present at the launch. "If it keeps up this initial speed and the same direction, it will reach the Pole in less than two days. The way to the

Andree was 42 years old and an explorer with ten years' polar experience when he announced his daring flight. No previous exploration generated the keen anticipation that his did.

Pole is clear, no more obstacles to encounter; the sea, the ice-field, and the Unknown!"

It was Andree's intention to fly to the Pole, land there, then travel back over the ice by sled; he had brought equipment and provisions in the basket of his balloon. It is sad to say, but must suffice: He was never seen alive again. Vilhjálmur Stefánsson, the renowned Arctic explorer and historian, author of *The Northward Course of Empire, Unsolved Mysteries of the Arctic* and many other books, theorized that Andree stayed aloft for three days before crash-landing on the ice at 83 degrees north latitude. Stefánsson recounted how Andree and his fellow adventurers made their way to White Island over the course of

three
arduous
months.
There, finally,
they died during
the brutally harsh winter of 1897-98.
Stefánsson based his account on the diaries,
logbooks and tentsite relics that were found
years later on the island.
And he based his tale on the messages of doves.

ANDREE HAD CARRIED thirty-six
homing pigeons aloft with him. Their
job was to transport news back to
Norway. We'll never know with
certainty how many birds he released during his two-
day flight, but it seems that there were at least three.

Andree, an able technician, oversaw the design of his mammoth balloon, the patching of its surface in the hangar at Spitzbergen and, of course, its north-ward launch.

Some experts contend that only one was found. Others insist: All three were.

The first to be located was picked up by a ship traveling north from the Barents Sea. Sure enough, there was a message in the canister attached to the bird's leg, and it read: "July 13, 12:30 midday. . . good speed to east. . . all well on board. This is the third pigeon-post."

Stefánsson wrote of the two "lost" doves: "Reports came

in that natives had killed a bird unknown to them (i.e., a pigeon) that they had eaten the bird and destroyed or lost a message which had been fastened to it. The excitement about the pigeons spread far and wide."

As well it might have, for stories began to circulate among the natives of Spitzbergen, Iceland and northern Norway and Sweden of an inexplicable discovery—a discovery nowhere mentioned in Stefánsson's careful writing. In Scandinavian histories written by indigenous people, the Sami, there is evidence that the second message was not "destroyed or lost" but in fact found months later on a Swedish beach. The extraordinary memorandum in that canister read (in translation): "July 11, 12:01 midnight... fast to north... fantastic sight, large mammals in flight... *deer?*... a hundred or more. This is the first pigeon-post."

A full year after Andree's balloon had taken off, another dead pigeon washed ashore at Victoria Island. It bore even more stunning information, as a tattered note now in the possession of the Artic Institute proves: "July 12, 11:00 midday... gust has blown us to 90 degrees north latitude... incredible vision, eyes are deceived! A crystal city below on the ice!... Shall investigate. This is the second pigeon post."

Although the messages were ignored at the time—not least because competitive English and American explorers didn't want to

Stefánsson was one of the century's most distinguished explorer-scientists, and ventured into the Arctic many times before his death in 1962.

admit that Andree might have been the first to fly over the Pole—the facts were recorded in scores of northern histories. These frank, unamazed narratives are not unlike the ones in the Inuit museum of Kuujjuaq.

"Again," says Oran Young, "*we're* the ones who are always astonished by this news of elves and other Arctic phenomena. The natives up there live with them and know them as neighbors. To them, this was no big deal. Elves and the flying deer, it's part of their daily culture. Want proof? Just look at old northern European paintings—not just the Inuit, Sami or other native stuff, either. You can see flying beasts in the distance just as surely as there are birds in American scenics. Why not? The deer were in training constantly, so of course they had become part of the landscape."

Just so. But as an historical item, the conclusions regarding Andree remain a very big deal to all of humankind. Think of it: Salomon Andree and his compatriots were the first men ever to view not only the North Pole *but also Santa Claus's kingdom*. Had they been able to land their balloon in those whirling winds above True North, they might have been the first men to make contact. As it was, all Andree was able to leave us was that alluring description, "a crystal city below on the ice!"

It's all but certain that the American adventurer Robert E.

Peary knew of Andree's sighting when he became the first man to reach the North Pole in 1909. After all, he had many Sami and Eskimos as members of his expedition, and they surely told him of Andree's two strange, suppressed messages. But just as surely, Peary himself saw nothing of Santa Claus. Peary was an ambitious man who sought fame as much as achievement itself. Had he discovered any sign of the elf nation, he unquestionably would have trumpeted the news. His silence remains the best evidence that he saw nothing.

"But Santa saw *him*," says Will Steger. "He told me so."

Steger, as far as is known, was the first person to actually venture into the elves' village, and remains the only person alive to have enjoyed this privilege. It is possible that an Inuit citizen or a Scandinavian adventurer also made his way into the sanctum, then kept the news largely to himself. There are legends of such things, particularly in the northern communities. But there is nothing written. And, most reliably, Steger reports that Santa Claus himself feels that his community has stayed a closed nation during its millennium on the Arctic ice. "Santa said I could talk about this when I returned to Minnesota," Steger says

Northerners say the second dove bore a missive from the balloon that eventually was found. The "July 12, 11:00 midday" note at the Arctic Institute bears them out.

12 juli, 11. för middag.

vindstøt har blåst os til 90
graders nord latitude...
utroligt syn, öynene er lurt,
en by av krystall på isen...
skal undersöke. Dette er
andren due post.

reflectively. "He said there were certain things it would be good for people to know.

"Where to start?" he continues. "Well, as I say, it was 1986 and eight of us were trying to get to the Pole by dogsled. We were attempting to be the first ones to do it by carrying our own supplies with us. On March eighth we went north onto the frozen polar sea from Drep Camp on the north coast of Ellesmere. Santa joked about that. He said he had taken the same route, a long, long time ago."

Steger remembers, "The first weeks were awful. The blocks of blue ice rose fifty feet or more, aligned like a series of huge frozen waves, and we had to climb each of these ridges with our tremendous loads. By the time we were nearing the Pole, in April, the ice was getting really weak and shifty—dangerous. After fifty days or so we were only a few miles from the top of the world, and things started getting strange. We heard odd noises, we hallucinated at times. This is to be expected in extreme conditions, but the things that we were thinking we saw. . .

"Once, it seems, the sky was filled with birds. They were so far off in the distance, yet we could see them. One of my teammates said, 'How could they be that big? We shouldn't be able to see an eagle from

The same route pioneered by Peary (above) in 1909 was followed by Will Steger years later (opposite).

here!' He shot some photos, hoping the animals could be identified later.

"Another time, I swore I saw man-made structures beyond an ice ridge. I shot some photos quickly, but by the time I had taken the camera down from my eye, whatever I had seen had vanished, like a mirage. 'Probably the shifting of the ice,' I said to myself.

"As we neared the Pole there was so much of that—moving ice, sudden loud cracks in the ice—that it was getting hazardous to travel fast as a team. We started scouting the safest routes individually, then doubling back to get the others. That's how the strangest, most wonderful day of my life began. It had warmed up to about minus-twenty, and there was a constant fog over the ice—very eerie and mysterious—and it was my turn to scout. I went out with Zap, my lead dog, and a team of eight, pulling a light sled—I wanted to travel nimbly over the ridges. We were making our way through this skim-milk haze, and every now and then a wind would blow an opening in the fog and I could see blue sky.

"Suddenly, I saw something. It was crazy. I saw this ice ridge ahead and what looked like a pinnacle above it, like a steeple. And then, just as suddenly as it had appeared, the fog enveloped it again.

STEGER'S 1986 INTERNATIONAL EXPEDITION TO THE NORTH POLE

SANTA'S VILLAGE

MAY 3: NORTH POLE

Steger's best estimate

MAY 1: 89°92'N 64°W

89°N

APRIL 27: 88°52'N 52°W

88°N

APRIL 24: 2ND SUSPECTED SIGHTING OF FLYING REINDEER

87°N

ARCTIC OCEAN

86°N

APRIL 16: 1ST SUSPECTED SIGHTING OF FLYING REINDEER

APRIL 11: 85°20'N 73°W   85°N

84°N

83°N

MARCH 8: ONTO THE POLAR ICE CAP

ELLESMERE

60 kilometers

"Now, in the Arctic, you can have visions all the time. I figured I had just had one. I said to myself, 'Will, it's the cold. It's been fifty days on the ice. You're seeing things.' I shook my head to get the cobwebs out, and drove the dogs toward the ice ridge, which wasn't a very high one. Maybe ten or fifteen feet tall.

"Zap started barking, just going nuts. He was making a racket all the way up the ridge, and soon all the other dogs started yapping too. I couldn't shut them up until Zap got to the top, and the minute he did he just stopped barking. Stopped cold. I had never seen that before—he always keeps barkin' when he senses something. But not this time. Zap was just struck dumb, and all the other dogs stopped too. So I'm pushing the sled up behind them and I'm shouting 'What's wrong, boy?

The pressure ridges, which sometimes climbed to fifty feet, made Steger's progress slow and exhausting.

What's up? What do you see?' Then I got to the top, and just as I did the fog blew away.

"There, below me, was heaven. It was Oz. It was the village itself."

STEGER STOPS TALKING and rises slowly. He goes down to the edge of the lake and looks out over the surface of the water. He walks back up the bank and slowly resumes his story, as he sits down again on a tree stump. As he talks, he continues to gaze out over the lake and struggles, briefly, to regain his composure.

"It was certainly the most beautiful thing I'd ever seen. The loveliest. The

strangest, of course, and. . . well, obviously it was the most unexpected." He smiles at this, then picks up steam. "It was both huge and small, if you can imagine that. A whole kingdom, and yet compact. A city of carefully sculpted snow and white-wood buildings that were all packed in tight, one against another. It was a booming metropolis, but it was just a village. It was a nation, but just a community. It was maybe three square miles, yet it was home to thousands—I could see them, scurrying around in the streets. It was overwhelming."

Steger says the village was "white—all white, pure white. The snow castles are white, the wooden factory is white, the streets aren't paved or shoveled because all travel

It wasn't until weeks later, when film was developed, that some of Steger's wildest notions of what he might have seen were confirmed.

is, of course, by reindeer. The reindeer are white! All the elves wear white. From December 26th until the following December 24th, Santa Claus himself wears white. The reason should be pretty obvious, pretty obvious,' this little elf told me."

Steger digresses briefly: "Well, they're all little, but this one was particularly short. His name sounded like Morluv, and he was the first one I met. 'Pretty obvious, pretty obvious, pretty obvious,' he kept saying—in English, once he had figured out which language I spoke. He speaks *dozens* of them. 'Pretty obvious, pretty obvious. I mean, well, it *should* be obvious. It's camouflage, you see. How do you hide in a tree? You do a green thing. In the desert? You do a brown thing. In the snow? You do a white thing! *Voila*— Here it is, here we are, the whitest white thing in the world! White on white on white on white on white!'

"He had surprised me," Steger continues. "He was up near the ridge, about a half mile from the village. He'd snuck up on me because he was as curious about me as I was about this amazing vision I had stumbled onto. He actually broke a law, I found out later. It's a rule in the village that if you see anything coming—anything at all—you're supposed to hide. But this Morluv was a fun-loving sort and really excitable. Hiding was the last thing on his mind. I guess he hadn't broken a law, exactly, because he wasn't punished—not while I was there. They just have these rules, and everybody obeys them. 'That way,' Santa told me later, 'everybody lives happily.' He then said, 'Tell your friends that. It works fine if you try.' "

S TEGER PAUSES AGAIN, picks a piece of grass from the bankside and starts chewing it. Now, the gleam of humor comes into his eyes. "I was there only a few hours, and Morluv became a great friend. They insinuate themselves into your affections, these elves. In ten minutes you feel like you've known them ten years. Morluv was a little crazy and a whole lot of fun. He was about two feet tall and said he was four hundred years old, more or less. 'In your *human* years,' he said, making it sound like dog years. He said four hundred was young, considering where he lived.

"Did you know," asks Steger, "that elves—or any animals, for that matter—live much longer at the Pole? It's true. It's the elf's physique and biology, and also the temperature. They're very small and efficient, and their

"Zap went through the whole range of emotions that day. He was afraid, he was exited, he was joyous. So was I."

– WILL STEGER,
*referring to his
longtime lead husky*

metabolism slows down to almost nothing because of the cold. Every minute that you live in New York City, an elf could do a full day's work. Every carrot they eat is roughly equivalent to three square meals for us.

"But anyway—I'm getting away from my story.

"He was about two feet tall, and he stunned me—I jumped a mile. He comes up and starts going crazy in elf language, elfese, or whatever— then tries French, German, Gaelic and about twenty other things on me before I hear him going 'Who're you? Who're you? Who're you???' And I say I'm Will Steger from Minnesota, and this doesn't mean too much to him, apparently. But he says this guy he knows—and then he gives the weird, elfin name for Santa—he says this guy must hear about this, and he puts his hand on the sled like he's going to guide it down into the village—like I'm a prisoner. And I'm thinking, 'This elf's two feet tall!' So I yank the sled away, even though I obviously want to go to the village. And you know what? The sled doesn't budge. Not a half-inch. I yank again. Nothing. The elf's two feet tall, maybe four hundred years old, and as strong as an ox. *Ten* oxen!

"So I mumble, 'Let's go.' He hops aboard, and we slide down into the village.

"At one point, Zap looked back and snarled at Morluv. Morluv smiled and went 'zzzzzzz.' Zap went quiet immediately, and seemed to like Morluv from that moment on. I learned while I was there that the elves have an uncommon, even uncanny way with animals. They love them, and are loved in return. It's principally between them and the reindeer, since that's the animal up there. But I'll tell you— my dogs didn't want to leave."

AT THE POLE · AS DESCRIBED BY WILL STEGER, 1986

RUNWAY~DETAIL

←————— 100 YARDS —————→

ARCTIC OCEAN
(ICE CAP)
NORTH POLE
75°
ELLESMERE I.
GREENLAND
SVALBARD
FRANZ JOSEF LAND
LAPTEV SEA

TRAINING CENTER

STABLES

RUNWAY

FACTORY

ELF VILLAGE

REINDEER ON TRAINING FLIGHT

CLAUS RESIDENCE

Everything is small. The elves are small, the reindeer are small, Santa is small. And therefore, the village is small. Only one mile in length by two in width, the entire town is tucked away—hidden behind ice ridges and by fog that swirls 'round the pole. On top of everything else, this elusive village is always moving. The polar ice cap is constantly shifting and drifting, and with it goes Santa's town. Today it is slightly west of true north, and tomorrow slightly south. Now it's floating east, now northwest. For anyone to have happened upon this place is a miracle, nothing but a miracle.

"NEITHER DID I, really, after what I saw up there," Steger continues. "And heard. And experienced. And learned. In two hours I got the most phenomenal education that you can imagine. My eyes were open wide, and I learned what the world can be.

"No, wait. What the world *is*. At its best place, right now."

Steger's thoughts return to the village: "What happened was, Morluv took me down into town, and I was walking down these narrow ice streets, watching all the elves go about their chores—their lives are nothing but chores, yet they love the chores." Steger smiles at the remembrance. "They're constantly grinning, and they always seem in an incredible hurry. They carry huge loads, and they hurry along. The streets are clogged with reindeer, too—the white ones, the Peary. They're everywhere, never harnessed. And the elves will be carrying loads of stuff, and they'll hop on a Peary and say, 'Heeeee!' and the thing will just bound out of sight. Incredible leaping ability! They just spring into the air, and disappear over the tops of these thin, ice-walled buildings.

"The most amazing thing about my visit was this—no one stared at me! No one cared about this 'man'—this man who was twice as big as any of them—walking down the street. They had jobs to do, places to get to. They smiled at me, and I tried to smile back. I was just so stunned by the whole experience, I couldn't be sure if I was smiling or laughing or crying.

"All the elves patted Zap and the other dogs as we walked down the main avenue. They said something that in the elfin tongue probably means dog. It sounded like 'Veeezaa.'

Morluv the elf, based upon a detailed description by Steger

Morluv was holding my hand as we went. He kept pointing out this and that, but he was excited too, and he kept slipping into elf language or Chinese or Spanish or something other than English. But finally I realized he was saying, 'Show you the place, show you the place!' "

The place was on the outskirts, "It was out by the farthest factory, which is beyond the farthest ice fields. The place was," Steger pauses. "Well, I would call it Reindeerland. There were hundreds of Peary out there, in stables and just roaming the ice. Some were feeding over by the greenhouses—the only non-white buildings up there because they're translucent. Other reindeer were out at the 'runway,' a hard-packed stretch of solid ice. At the runway, Peary were taking off, one after another. They would start, then they would be a blur as they went down the runway—a speck you could barely see, a spark shooting along. And then there was a flash of light, and you saw the spark disappear into the blue sky. One after another they went. So fast, so fine. I'll admit it—it brought tears to my eyes.

"Above us, gliding, were a hundred reindeer—two hundred, five hundred! They coated the sky. They were cruising, then sprinting, then—*whoooooosh!*—going into overdrive. You can recognize them as reindeer only when they coast through the sky. When they *really* fly, they just look like a flash of light. They seemed so fast to me, but Morluv kept saying, 'Those aren't the good ones. Those aren't the good ones. Those aren't the good ones.' "

The "good ones," the ones that we know—Dasher, Dancer and the gang—were in a grand stable behind the

The Greenhouse

REINDEER CORRAL NEAR AIRFIELD

runway, Steger reports. "They were attended by a hundred elves, bringing corn and carrots from the greenhouses," he says. "Seemed to me they were really pampered. They have this nice, cushy, kind of regal stable—and all the other deer sleep outside. I asked if the good ones were in the stable just then, and Morluv nodded vigorously. 'Resting, resting, resting,' said Morluv, 'resting, resting.'

"It was spring, of course, when I was there. As I was soon to learn—from Santa himself, in fact—the nine deer who make the annual journey must rest a full four months before they start to train for the next year's Mission. The short of it is, they burn out. They go so hard for one night, and then just collapse. Time is just different up there, that's all there is to it. They're different animals, living in the same world as us but living by their own rules. To them, it all makes sense."

Steger adds: "Morluv and I left the reindeer training grounds and headed back into the village. I had so many questions to ask, when Morluv stunned me by saying, 'Want to meet? Want to meet? Want to meet?' I asked, 'Who?' He said, 'Him,' and then he said that weird fa-la-la name. I said, 'Santa?' He laughed uncontrollably, nodding up and down like a maniac. 'Yesyesyesyesyesyes,' he said. 'Sandra Claus! Him you call Sandra Claus!!'

"He took my hand, turned me around once more and led me on."

S TEGER STOPS FOR A MOMENT, and looks at the sky. He is thinking. He looks at the ground, and says slowly, "Santa said I could relate certain things, and others I should not tell. I was surprised by how open he was, and how much information he wanted me to

"I can say unequivocally that the villagers are the most industrious people on earth. I mean, elves on earth."

– EINAR GUSTAVSSON,
*Icelandic scholar and
elf historian*

bring back. He seemed to want to seize this rare opportunity—as I did, of course. He said I could say that the village is peaceful, that the village is unarmed, that the village is there for the good of all mankind, that the village loves all countries and all the children of all the countries, that the village will never perish, that the village will never desert us. He added that the village is movable, but there was a twinkle in his eye, and I didn't know how to take that. I'm not sure what he meant."

Steger continues: "He lives in a house—not a castle—out by the reindeer grounds. He does have a wife, yes, and, interestingly, they have two children."

A quick word about the Claus family: Mrs. Claus is an often mentioned woman in northern lore, so even before Steger gave evidence there was good reason to believe in her existence. Gleaning from various traditions, we can assume she is an able administrator who focuses on local matters while Santa Claus oversees the global operation. "Seems to me, she runs the Pole," says Steger. Mrs. Claus is in charge of the factories, which are in operation twenty-four hours each day, 364 days a year. Einar Gustavsson, the Icelander who envisioned Santa's flight from Greenland and is an expert on all aspects of elfin society, says this is in no way unusual for a community of elves. "They are by far the best workers in the world," he says. "This is because our ideas of time spent well and time spent poorly are inverted in an elfin society. Work is fun to them. Watching television is not fun. They love to go to work. I would presume the factories of the North Pole are turning out product at about a half ton an hour,

and I would presume this makes those factory workers pretty pleased and proud."

Neither of the Claus children works in the factory. "They're not lazy," Steger says. "They're just outdoorsy." The boy is an able reindeer trainer; the girl's an exercise rider. In fact, she is the one who takes large teams of Peary on thousand-mile midnight flights, to work on their technique and stamina. "Mrs. Claus is awfully proud of the daughter," says Steger. "It seems the girl is just about the best reindeer jockey in five hundred years." It's interesting to note: The "girl" is, herself, perhaps 300 or 400 years old—if we can extrapolate from references to the children in Sami histories.

"We shared tea and cookies, using silverware with a Santa pattern," says Steger of his visit to the household. "I think cookies are the national food up there, everyone's always eating cookies— the Pole is on one big sugar fix. Anyway, we shared tea and cookies by Santa's fire, and he talked with me. He was a little chagrined at first when Morluv brought me to the door. But, as his wife explained to me, elves do not stay chagrined. Chagrined, mad, angry, vengeful—these are foreign to them. They shed these emotions like a winter coat in springtime."

Steger's voice indicates that his tale is reaching a close: "As I say, he told me a lot. He told me, very succinctly, why he did what he did—'Out of love'—but he would not tell me when he started, nor what prompted him to start. He told me how hard it is on the deer, not to mention the elves. But he felt that all of his faithful— the elves *and* the deer—did the work because they wanted to. He told me. . ."

The tea service reflected the Claus family's good cheer and sly humor.

HE TOLD STEGER A LOT, and told him to bring the message south—minus the few precious secrets that must never be revealed. Santa Claus was, by accounts, a gracious host as he sat there in his long underwear, sipping his tea, gently petting the head of a young Peary caribou that rested by his feet. Steger laments that he had not brought his camera from camp: "It was only supposed to be an hour's scouting trip!" But then he reconsiders and says he is happy he didn't have it, happy that the marvelous experience exists only in the warmth of memory. "It's interesting, when we got back to America and developed the film from other parts of our trip to the Pole, the photos confirmed that we *had* seen strange things in the sky. In certain frames there are small but undeniable unidentified flying objects. I'm certain—now—that these were the reindeer." Steger told Claus as he departed, "I'd love to have my friends meet you." Claus answered, "Yes, wonderful, that would be pleasant." And so Steger and Zap headed back to camp excitedly. They found the others without problem. Steger gathered his compatriots in a lathered rush, and the eight of them pointed their dog teams due north.

They searched and searched but never saw sign of Santa Claus, his village or any flying reindeer. On the fifty-fifth day of their expedition they reached the Pole: True North. Still nothing. When Steger traveled to the Pole again in 1995, he traveled an empty expanse. Nothing.

But. . . he *knew* that the ice cap was not the white void it seemed. He felt the presence. He saw nothing, but he felt. . . *something.*

"The dogs were never bothered by the reindeer flying overhead," says Steger. "They were northern dogs, and seemed to understand."

PART THREE

The Miracle of Reindeer Flight

Mysteries Explained, Science Revealed

D ESPITE FIRSTHAND testimony, some people still doubt. "Really?" they ask. "Do they *really* fly?" Well, we shouldn't feel shy about asking, we shouldn't feel bad about disbelieving. The fact is, debate has raged forever, not just among children but among scientists as well.

HILLARY &
TENZING ~ 1953
S.E. RIDGE ~ EVEREST

MAMMALOGISTS HAVE BEEN FIGHTING for years about whether it's true flight or what some of them used to call extended leaping," says zoologist Tony Vecchio. Vecchio is director of the Roger Williams Park Zoo in Providence, Rhode Island. Only recently, he says, have scientists and Santalogists agreed that reindeer are, in fact, flying. And news of this codification in the ranks of techno-thinkers has been slow to spread. Many people you pass on the street, day in and day out, still do not believe.

"And that's really too bad," Vecchio continues. "Because the flying deer is just about the most astounding animal in the world. He should be believed in, he also should be looked up to. Santa's team of eight— plus, of course, the one with the nose—they are perfect mammals. They are unique and beautiful, not to say miraculous. They're the pinnacle of evolution."

━

ALTHOUGH WE KNOW that the Peary caribou is the true flier, many species of reindeer can *sort of* fly. A 600-pound woodland caribou in Canada can clear a river with a jump and glide, thanks to its extremely elastic tendons and other characteristics that it shares with the Peary. But it is only the Peary that can travel long distances and that can actually climb to high altitude. The Peary is the one that "mounts to the sky."

The question is: How?

"*Rangifer tarandus pearyi* is closely related to the larger reindeer but is a singular animal," says Bil Gilbert, our naturalist from Pennsylvania who has written extensively on Arctic fauna for *Smithsonian* and other magazines. "A Peary weighs only a hundred-fifty

> "This particular reindeer, known as the Peary, is not a miracle. But it is something close to a miracle."
>
> – TONY VECCHIO,
> *zoologist and animal biologist*

pounds—that's where the 'eight tiny reindeer' thing comes from. It's the smallest deer in the world, and if you looked at it alongside a moose, an elk or even a regular white-tailed deer, you'd never guess they were related."

Perhaps, but lots of flightless things are small. What else is there?

"Well, as the northernmost deer in the world," continues Gilbert, "the Peary is awfully hardy and strong. You can imagine how tough it is to survive at those latitudes up there, with that weather—the cold, those vicious winds. But Peary thrive there. They have a phenomenal strength-to-weight ratio, the greatest of all mammals by about three times. It's such a strange little deer, a lot of people don't understand it, and therefore they don't believe in it."

━

AS YOU MIGHT IMAGINE, the Peary isn't commonly seen. Tiny as it is, camouflaged in its snow-white coat, based in a habitat that is forbidding in the extreme, it has developed an almost mystical reputation: *Does it really even exist?* In this sense of borderline reality, the Peary is a member of a fascinating, semi-mythical menagerie of beasts that seem to fall somewhere between truth and illusion. The ocean-going narwhal and the Himalayan snow leopard can be seen as the Peary's animal-kingdom cousins. In his 1978 book *The Snow Leopard*, Peter Matthiessen tells of an Asian Lama, Milarepa, who, "to confound his enemies, resorted to his black Nyingma-pa Tantra (magic) and transformed himself into a snow leopard at Lachi-Kang (Mount Everest)." And in his best-selling *Arctic Dreams*, the equally esteemed Barry Lopez writes of the narwhal, "No large

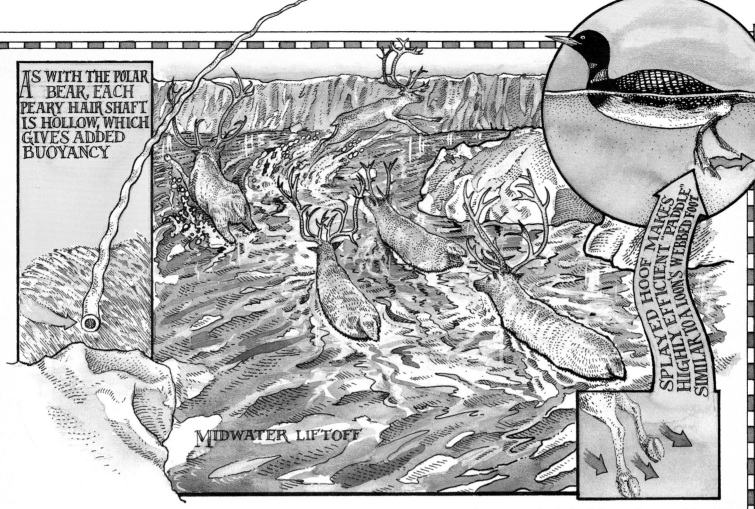

AS WITH THE POLAR BEAR, EACH PEARY HAIR SHAFT IS HOLLOW, WHICH GIVES ADDED BUOYANCY

MIDWATER LIFTOFF

SPLAYED HOOF MAKES HIGHLY EFFICIENT "PADDLE" SIMILAR TO A LOON'S WEBBED FOOT

mammal in the Northern Hemisphere comes as close as the narwhal to having its very existence doubted. . . .We know more about the rings of Saturn than we know about the narwhal." Magic and rumor—so it goes with the Peary. Yet all of these species are certifiably real; they are *not* just so many Sasquatches. What mystique they possess is attributable to their exotic looks, to their elusiveness and to the quasi-spiritual regions where they dwell.

"Everyone asks about the Peary's magic," says Gilbert. "It's such an odd creature, people ascribe all sorts of things to it. It lives such a long time that people say it's immortal. It is not. Many Peary can fly, so some scientists insist it's a bird and not a mammal. Hardly. A bat is a mammal, and a bat flies. In fact, a bat's gliding mechanism is very similar to a Peary's. Many Peary live on the ice cap, so some people speculate that it subsists on snow. Nonsense. The Peary

A maneuver such as this demonstrates how the Peary is constantly using all of its unique physical attributes to better advantage.

needs precious little food, but it does need food."

Other legends dispelled: There are those who say it is a superdeer brought to earth by Saint Nicholas for his purposes only. Simply not true. Nicholas—or whoever he is—has been adept at harnessing the Peary to his needs, and at breeding Peary. But if these are just 'Santa's deer,' then why aren't they *all* on the ice cap? Why have they been photographed on Ellesmere, been seen also at the Kane Basin on Greenland, at Hyperit Point on Axel Heiberg Island, on North Devon Island, on Prince Patrick Island, on Meighen Island? They are all over the place up there, and in number. There are, perhaps, a half million Peary on earth, approximately ninety-five percent of which live or migrate above the Arctic Circle. Gilbert enumerates other characteristics of the breed: "They're built for the cold and wind. They're low to the ground, strong and sure-footed. Those in Santa Claus's village are also particularly suited for the dicey proposition of living on an ice cap. How so? Well, like all reindeer, they are absolutely phenomenal swimmers. Their hair is hollow in the center which gives them buoyancy, and their large splayed hooves make for terrific paddles. So if the surface ice cracks beneath them in summer, they can churn back to the shelf and clamber up. They can even go into a mid-water liftoff like a huge duck if they want to exert the effort. I've seen that happen on Ellesmere. It's the most sensational thing I've ever been witness to. It is something that just takes your breath away."

T HE PEARY CARIBOU IS REAL, and the Peary caribou can fly. But again, *how* does it fly?

"It is actually easier to comprehend than it is to believe," says Gilbert, whose book *How Animals Communicate* shows an uncanny understanding of the motives and desires of wildlife. "Let me explain it to you."

Gilbert proceeds to do so: "I think the most important aspect of all is willpower. It's like with a great athlete—if he has the tools, great, but does he have the drive and desire to get the most out of these tools? The truly successful flying deer, certainly including the ones used by Santa, must have tremendous intestinal fortitude."

Gilbert goes on to explain how all reindeer and caribou are splay-hooved, and this creates a large surface area useful for all kinds of walking, running and thrusting: "Physically, the two most important aspects of a flier are the hooves and the antlers." After centuries of living in snow-covered lands, the North Pole Peary has developed a hoof every bit as big as that of a St. George's herd caribou. This acts as a kind of snowshoe when he's on the

> "The Peary is the Babe Ruth of reindeer. It has innate talent, a yearning to be the best and an unquenchable joie de vivre."
>
> – BIL GILBERT,
> *naturalist and author*

ground, and in the air it acts as a small, solid wing. "Trust me," says Gilbert, "it's a big hoof for a little deer. It's as if you had size-fifty feet. Try thinking of it that way."

The hoof must not only be large and flat on the bottom but also streamlined from toe to heel. It's rather like the wing of an airplane in this way, and creates the same effect. What's at work here is called Bernoulli's principle, and has to do with air rushing over a flat surface, thus creating loft. "It's pretty technical," says Gilbert, "and I won't bore you with that part."

A LSO IMPORTANT is antler configuration. "Let me start by saying that reindeer are the only antlered animal on earth to have a tined forehead at the base of the antler—it's a protruding, bony forehead," Gilbert informs us. "On a big reindeer it seems like a little bump, but on the Peary it seems like a massive shelf sticking up from his head. For him, when in flight, it's like a spinnaker on a sailboat—it's an extra sail, banking the wind up and over. *Whooosh!* And it has other practical applications. When the deer is on the ground, the tine can be used as a shovel. A lot of reindeer use it this way when foraging for lichen and other moss on the snow-covered tundra. But consider how it might help the Peary on Santa's traveling squad. They can get out of any bad-weather mess they might encounter, or can clear the way to a window or chimney in two seconds flat. The tine also keeps snow out of their eyes, even when flying through blizzard conditions."

Gilbert's talking fast and clearly enjoying himself. "Another thing about the antlers—reindeer are one of only three kinds of deer in the world to develop the

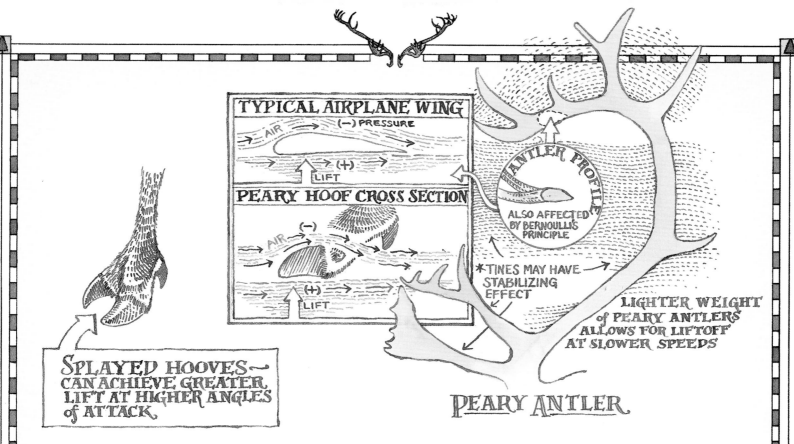

TYPICAL AIRPLANE WING

AIR → (−) PRESSURE

LIFT

PEARY HOOF CROSS SECTION

AIR (−)

(+)

LIFT

ANTLER PROFILE
ALSO AFFECTED BY BERNOULLI'S PRINCIPLE

* TINES MAY HAVE STABILIZING EFFECT

LIGHTER WEIGHT OF PEARY ANTLERS ALLOWS FOR LIFTOFF AT SLOWER SPEEDS

SPLAYED HOOVES CAN ACHIEVE GREATER LIFT AT HIGHER ANGLES OF ATTACK

PEARY ANTLER

palmated, or broad-ended type of horn. This too creates wind resistance, and thus loft.[4] So they're in the air. But now comes a curious thing: If a bird species can fly, all members can fly. Same for bats—there are no earth-bound bats. But among Peary, only certain ones can take off and fly for any length of time. Why?"

He waits for the guess, which doesn't come. He offers it: "Because at a hundred-fifty, two hundred pounds, they're a pretty large bird, a pretty big bat. And, apparently, only one pattern of antler allows for extended flight. This one complex configuration creates a vortex of wind at high speeds. The perfect rack acts as a big mainsail, lifting the beast heavenward. With nine sails out and a takeoff speed of about eight hundred miles an hour at the end of the runway, Santa's team would have liftoff power equivalent to several jet planes—and it would

A Peary interacts with wind currents very much as an airplane or hang-glider does, encouraging lift and float.

[4] The other two types of palmated-antler animals—the moose and the fallow deer—are much too big for flying. As Gilbert says: "The Peary is the lucky one, with everything in proportion."

be about a hundredth the size of a Boeing 747.

"You see what I mean?"

There is incidental testimony concerning how many Peary are good fliers. Adventurers who have traveled across Ellesmere Island have said that a huge herd of migrating reindeer will have perhaps one or two deer floating above it, with others occasionally springing into the air for brief flights. (Gilbert is in possession of an old, presumably top-secret U.S. government photograph that seems to confirm this rarely witnessed phenomenon.) Wendy Williams, who runs a reindeer ranch outside Anchorage, Alaska, claims to know the ratio of fliers to non-fliers with some precision and relates an amazing tale. "Santa told us one in a thousand Peary can really fly," Williams says, stating that she was visited by Claus in 1989 when he was on a scouting trip. "He was looking for athletic deer to add to his stable. He selected one of our young Peary named Turbo. He said the kid had potential and might be a flier one day."

Williams says that it was painful to part with Turbo,

one of her cutest deer. "But it was for Santa, and for such a good cause. When Santa asks, what can you say? Of course you say yes. By all means—Yes! I mean, we were so shocked at even seeing him here, all we could say was, 'Yessir, yessir.' I suppose in the lower forty-eight the shock would've been even greater. Up here we hear of him coming 'round, and we know about elves. But still, I was pretty surprised.

"You know," she adds, "I should mention, Santa looks *great* in the summer. That's when he does these recruiting missions, in the summer, because in the spring he's exhausted and in the fall and winter he's simply too busy. He told us that summer is his only downtime all year.

"But as I was saying, he looked great—trimmer than you'd expect and very fit. He even had a bit of a tan, though his cheeks were certainly still rosy. I felt the same way you feel whenever you see a famous person, that he's not nearly as big as you think he's going to be. In fact, I'd say Santa's tiny. A little guy, but an awfully nice man.

"There's one thing I regret not asking. To this day, I can't figure out how he got here. Then, before I knew it, he was gone. I'd love to know if he flew in, or if maybe one of his reindeer brought him over, and landed in the highlands. He's a mysterious little fellow, that's for sure. But nice. Very nice. And he does *such* a good job. Amazing, when you think about it."

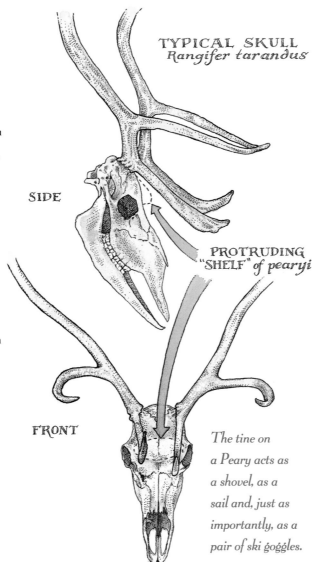

TYPICAL SKULL
Rangifer tarandus

SIDE

PROTRUDING "SHELF" *of pearyi*

FRONT

The tine on a Peary acts as a shovel, as a sail and, just as importantly, as a pair of ski goggles.

WILLIAMS, speaking from experience, says the food you give a reindeer is crucial to its performance. Zookeeper Vecchio of Providence concurs, and says timing would be just as important for Santa Claus: He must put out certain foods at certain times of the year.

"Most reindeer breeders wouldn't have to worry about things like that, they could just keep their animals on a normal diet all year," says Vecchio. "Because it really doesn't matter if the animals perform better on December 24th or on the Fourth of July, right? But Santa's got a different problem. His reindeer have to peak like an Olympic swimmer, and therefore they must bulk up and taper down—just like an Olympic swimmer."

Without being clued, Vecchio correctly surmises that the traveling squad does no heavy work until summer. "An effort like they have to put forth," he says as he inspects the cheetah cage at Roger Williams Park Zoo, "I'd bet they just about hibernate all spring. Maybe they limber up every now and then, but no muscle building. If they move a muscle at all, it's probably in their jaws—they're yawning, snoring, eating or telling tales about the big night. 'You shoulda seen the quicksand Dasher almost landed us in!' That kinda thing.

"They're gettin' fat, is what I mean."

H E MOVES on to the tiger cage, and continues with the scenario. "I would assume that on a two-hundred-pound animal who's gonna have to do what these guys are gonna have to do, the layer of fat gets up to about four inches. Easy. So they're plump

the kinda guy that doesn't use a whip, so he probably says, like a football coach, 'Okay you sluggos, the party's over!' And now the drills start.

"I'm sure the workouts are different for different deer. The fast

When Gilbert found this photograph buried in U.S. Agriculture Department files, he wondered why he—or anyone else—had never seen it before.

little Peary by the time summer rolls around. I'll bet they get some ribbing about that, when they come outta the stables.

"Anyway, they're overweight—fat and happy.

"So now, Santa cracks the whip. Except I assume he's

ones do wind sprints, the big lugs do distance—that sort of thing. I'm equally sure that the nine hotshots don't work out by themselves. I'll bet Santa's got a huge support system, a big team of reindeer that's always pushing the superstars. It's like anything, right? You need competition to stay on top.

"So I'm guessing, July, these guys are doing maybe ten

thousand miles in the air, twenty thousand on the ground, with takeoff and hopping exercises intermixed. August, those figures are tripled. September, the big guys are training on their own, 'cause the others just can't keep up. They're doing phenomenal mileage now—a million miles a month. They're taking off on solo California-and-back training runs, just for practice. They probably spend a week at the equator, getting used to heat again. Santa's very lucky that reindeer are his thing. They've got this blood-circulation system that's ideal for a cold-adapted animal. I'll give you some science stuff—the system's sim-

the heart itself doesn't overheat! I'll tell you, the only two animals in the wide, wide world that could pull that sleigh are a reindeer or a great big blubbery flying Blue Whale!"

VECCHIO FINDS HIMSELF at the reindeer cage. In the ninety-degree-heat of a Rhode Island summer, the animal inside looks serene. "See this guy?" says Vecchio. "He's got maybe an inch of fat on him. That's about where the Super Eight are in maybe October. Well, the Super Nine. Whatever.

"They're down to an inch of fat, but they're even *heavier* than they were in spring! Pure muscle. They've been eating like hogs, and it's all going to muscle—exactly where three inches of the spring roll has already gone. If reindeer were mean by nature, I'd say at this point—Stay clear! But they're not, they're just serious. They're focused. No nonsense now, no reminiscing, no past glories. They sleep, they get up, they eat, they work out,

ilar to the *rete mirabile* system which means 'miraculous bundles,' and in this system the small arteries and veins are intertwined so that cool blood from the appendages—the legs, I mean—is warmed by the arterial flow—the blood from the heart. Deep-diving whales have got *rete mirabile*, and reindeer have something similar. Lucky for Mr. Claus.

"But anyway, here's the cool part. The miracle bundles work as a heater at a hundred-below, or as an air conditioner at a hundred-above. Why? Because

Wildlife photographer Jim Brandenburg spent a summer watching young Peary train on Ellesmere Island. These cousins of Claus's deer are still waiting for their antlers to grow.

they eat, they nap, they work out, they eat, they work out, they eat, they go to bed. All day they see the elves carting the toys around—they get inspired. Santa looks out on the whole thing and he smiles.

"November—serious crunch time. I would guess that, by now, they've got their distance training all set. They've got their miles in. Did you ever think about The Christmas Mission? I have. Flying's just the half of it. There's the big long glide to start, and the big expanses from Australia to Asia, California

THE REINDEER YEAR

MINIMAL EXERCISE

RECOVERY PERIOD

NEAR HIBERNATION - REST, FEED, BUILD UP BODY FAT

JANUARY | **FEBRUARY** | **MARCH**

NEW TRAINEES INTRODUCED

FLIGHT PLANS - CHANGES DISCUSSED

"FAT & HAPPY"

APRIL | **MAY** | **JUNE**

AIR ~ 10,000 miles
GROUND ~ 20,000 miles

EXERCISE INCREASES X 3

SOLO ROUND TRIPS TO CALIFORNIA

JULY | **AUGUST** | **SEPTEMBER**

STRICT REGIMEN
• EXERCISE
• DIET
• SLEEP

FAT CALIPER

DOWN TO 1 INCH BODY FAT

AGILITY DRILLS

• ANXIOUS
• SLEEPLESS
FAT CONTENT NEAR ZERO

- READY TO GO...

OCTOBER | **NOVEMBER** | **DECEMBER**

to Hawaii, Ireland to Canada and so forth. But, really, most of the night is spent hopping. Bouncing from house to house in the same neighborhood, or maybe going from, like, Providence to Pawtucket—which is, of course, nothing for them.

"So my guess is, November is spent doing agility drills. I'll bet they're bouncin' off the ice all month like they were just big Jack Russell terriers. Did you know reindeer have the most elastic tendons in the animal kingdom? It's true. You can look it up."

Now it's December," Vecchio continues. "It's December, and it's a pretty exciting time for these guys. They're trying to sleep, but they can't. They're rarin' to go, but they can't—not yet. Their fat content is minimal, and their muscle mass is enormous. They are *there*.

"Santa tries to calm them. He probably visits them nightly. Let's face it, there's no coach in the world better than he is—not at this stuff.

"So he tells them, 'Well, gang, here we go again. We've. . . .' Well, I won't try to guess what he'd say. He'd be sure to say the perfect thing. I'm a zoo guy, I should stick to the animals."

Vecchio concludes: "But I was saying, about the deer—the deer are bulked, pumped and ready to go. And since the Pole is dark all day long on December 24th, I envision this amazing midnight-black sendoff, with a solemn prayer maybe, then Santa climbing aboard, then a whistle, fifty thousand cheering—not to mention exhausted—elves, and then a

snort from Dasher and—bang, *zooooooom!*—the team is out of sight, a fireball disappearing to the southeast.

"So that's my reindeer year. I'd love to run it by Santa, see what he thinks, see if I got it right. I'd love to know."

Santa Claus, of course, is not available for queries. But while Claus isn't answering questions, Will Steger is. Presented with Vecchio's scenario, which touches on many points Steger put to the elf himself, he says simply, "Impressive." After rubbing his rough beard a few times, he adds, "I'd say that's just about right."

Peary caribou, while ferociously hardy, are not indefatigable. Not even Vecchio's "hotshots" can go all night without replenishment. Like any animal, they need some rest and food when engaged in extended exercise.

On their big night, Santa's team requires near-constant attention, and much of the succor comes at home. During each of their 1,756 returns to the North Pole, the reindeer are unhitched by a crack team of elves and they are fed and washed. While other elves refill the sleigh with gifts, the deer's legs are rubbed, their hooves checked. Santa, too, takes in food during the lightning-fast stopovers, and he changes red suits between 500 and 600 times each Christmas Eve. If he's returning from Africa, the sweat is a problem. If he's coming in from London, it's the soot.

Even with the Polar pit stops, the reindeer do tire.

One of the 500–600 red suits Santa changes into each Christmas Eve. This one, based on a West Greenland whaler design, is one piece to save time. Santa enters through a hole in the middle and draws string tight.

Mittens & leggings are removable on some suits for southern hemisphere flights.

"Santa told me he has rest areas all around the world," says Steger. "Now, understand, a rest for these guys is about ten seconds—they bounce back so quickly it's amazing. But they do have these places set up, usually at the highest altitudes, where they have stashed food and water. The elves go out in late autumn to stock these caches. It's a very orderly, sophisticated operation."

According to Steger, it was long, long ago—in the very first years of the annual Mission—that Claus determined his team could not service the great expanse of Asia, for instance, or the distant continents of the Southern Hemisphere, without replenishment. Each November for nearly 2,000 years, reconnaissance missions of elves on reindeerback have flown the far-flung skies, readying the world to receive its gift-giver. Their cargo is mostly slow-burning, high-fat foods. It includes exotica like muktuk from North Atlantic whales and jerky from Lapland elk, as well as the reindeer staples: cracked barley, fishmeal, cottonwood sawdust for fiber, molasses for fast-twitch energy, salt. The elves secure these things in wood-and-metal casks that are buried in snow near the summits of mountains. These peaks are the prominent

Upon returning to Buenos Aires, the flyer Henri Guillaumet (center) explained to the press that he had survived in the Andes on "found food."

ones, instantly recognizable from on high. Any pilot can pick these singular mountains out of a dense range, and Santa Claus is not just any pilot.

Steger's testimony serves to confirm many reports brought back from mountaineering expeditions through the years—reports of strange findings on summits that had never before been visited by man. In a famous incident involving Antoine de St. Exupery's storied Aeropostale service of the early 1930s, the young pilot Henri Guillaumet crash-landed on a frozen lake during a storm in Argentina's Andes Cordillera Range, where some mountains are higher than 21,000 feet. Guillaumet trekked for days, defying the wisdom that "the Andes don't give men back." He was finally found in the foothills by a group of Argentine gauchos. He was ravaged by cold and exhaustion, and was in a delirium. But he was alive.

"*Impossible*," St. Exupery thought, when told of Guillaumet's survival. "*C'est incroyable!*" Guillaumet claimed to have found food in the highest heights of the Andes. "Food from heaven!" he told his friend. "I thought you had dropped the crate for me, Saint Ex!" His assertion was seen as the raving of an unstabilized man, yet even after he fully recovered, Guillaumet clung stubbornly to his story. His colleagues began to wonder, *What did he find up there?*

I ASKED SANTA about the Everest rumors," says Steger. "He smiled, and said, 'Yes, sure—that was the first stop I ever used. I've been using it for years.'" There had been stories and legends about this for decades: That something strange was going on at the top of the world's highest mountain. Tibetans and Nepalese who live in the shadow of the great peak have long felt that someone—or some*thing*—was at work up there, particularly in late autumn and early winter. In fact, for four decades rumors have circulated in the mountaineering community that the most famous climber in history actually found evidence of a Claus cache on Everest. Even now, all these years after his monumental achievement, Sir Edmund Hillary will not confirm the stories.

But he will not quite deny them, either.

Speaking from his home in Auckland, New Zealand, Sir Edmund, who is today 77 years old and still in fine fettle, talks guardedly but warmly about those dramatic days in 1953 when he and his Sherpa climbing compan-

> "I sometimes wonder what happened to the offering that Tenzing made at the top of Everest."
>
> – SIR EDMUND HILLARY, *mountain climber and living legend*

ion, Tenzing Norgay—who died in India in 1987 at the age of 72—thrilled the world by becoming the first men to successfully climb Everest. Adding new information to the Everest story for the first time in forty years, Sir Edmund addresses the Santa Claus questions squarely, while emphasizing that evidence has always remained elusive.

"The Buddhist monks in the Tengboche Monestery at the foot of Mount Everest gave us their blessing for the success of our climb," says Sir Edmund, who in the decades after that climb became a hero to those Buddhists by founding schools and hospitals throughout the region. "The Head Lama pointed out his belief that some of their gods often spent a little time on the summit of the mountain, and asked us not to disturb them."

Sir Edmund pauses, then recalls the climactic day. "Six weeks later, Sherpa Tenzing and I labored up the last steep slopes and emerged on the summit of the mountain. What an exciting moment that was!

"I looked carefully around—no sign of humans and no sign of gods. But Tenzing was placing some small cookies and some chocolate in a small hole in the snow. Was it food for his gods or maybe Santa himself?

"I never did ask him that question!"

N ED GILLETTE, an adventurer who lives in Sun Valley, Idaho, and reached Everest's 29,028-foot summit himself in 1992, says he found what Hillary and Tenzing must have missed by inches. "I literally stumbled onto the box," says Gillette. "I was the last one on our team as we made our way over the Hillary Step and up towards the peak. The guy in front of me on the rope

After Tenzing (above, left) and Hillary made their final push to the peak in 1953, Tenzing posed, then proceeded to bury this big metal canister filled with Nepalese chocolates.

kicked some snow away, and there it was. It wasn't all that big. Maybe three feet by two, I would guess. I didn't know what it was, though of course I'd heard the rumors about Hillary and Norgay and Santa. I thought, 'Maybe this is the food storage. Maybe it's true!'

"I looked around, and I'll tell you something interesting. Just below the Step, just southwest of the summit, there's a little hollow—a half-moon crescent of flat rock tucked in against the cliff. You could stand there, four or five men could stand there. It wouldn't be a bad place for a rest. And then I imagined it—the sleigh coming through the night sky, Santa seeing the highest peak on earth, banking his sleigh gently and circling down toward the mountain. The whole great team, taking a rest as the stars in the heavens create a firestorm in the black sky. It was a lovely vision."

When the Santa Claus express is traveling at top speed, it seems but a streak.

A LOVELY VISION, TO BE SURE—and lovely thoughts must be in Claus's head each year as he descends toward Everest. But he would not be floating out of the sky in quite so lyrical a fashion as Gillette describes. Perhaps if you saw him during a leisurely training run in early August you might be able to discern the sleigh and reindeer, or perhaps if you captured him in freeze-frame you could see a calmly sailing Santa Claus. But if you saw him on Christmas Eve, you would see nothing but a blur. He zooms, *zooms*, all night long. If you've seen a shooting star on December 24th, it might not have been a shoot-

ing star. It might have been Santa Claus, zooming.

The statistics tell the tale: Claus must travel nearly 75 million miles each December 24-25, his team progressing at a rate of 650 miles per second—many times the speed of sound, though of course not near the speed of light.[5] Even at such a phenomenal rate, Claus needs all the darkness that the night of December 24-25 can afford. Thanks to the rotation of the earth, and the fact that the more populous Northern Hemisphere is in its season of longest nights, he has not twenty-four but a full thirty-one hours to work with. "He uses all of it," says Oran Young. "Every second. In fact, at the westernmost edge of the dateline, those islands in the Pacific are loaded with reports of someone or something banging around at dawn, creating a ruckus. He's not a vampire, after all, and there are lots and lots of people who swear they've seen him in daylight."

"He told me he has gotten better at the operation over the years," says Steger. "But he said, 'Then again, I *had* to.'"

What Claus was alluding to is the way civilization has changed in 2,000 years. "The first few years, Santa was finding his way," says Steger. "In fact, early on, he did *not* visit the entire world. And once he decided to visit everybody, he took several nights in December to do so. Then

[5] This information derives from an experiment conducted by Oran Young of Dartmouth's Arctic Institute, along with college photographer Joe Mehling, during Claus's flyover of New Hampshire in 1991. Mehling's photography and an explanation of the experiment can be seen on page 73.

-70-

Gillette made his way over the Hillary Step (bottom) and was about to press on for the summit when he stumbled upon the cache (top). "It was unquestionably Santa's," he says. "It even was marked with an emblem." Gillette did not open the box, and reburied it immediately after a fellow climber recorded the find on film.

he got better at it, the reindeer got better and faster, the training methods were improved, the shuttling back to the Pole for more gifts became smoother. The planning of his route became more and more sophisticated. Santa has extraordinary navigational skills, and his main hobby is cartography. In back of his house he has a bunker he calls the map room. The walls are covered with maps of the earth, and there are hundreds of books that he has compiled himself on celestial navigation, lunar navigation, oceanic navigation—you name it. In the map room he has shelves filled with airline schedules, mountain altitudes, climates in all zones of the planet. He has everything."

WHERE DID HE GET THOSE materials that he didn't create himself? From "Santa's Helpers." Says Young: "It's not an organization, it's not a fraternity, it's not a club. It is a loosely organized network of specialists around the globe who do what they can to make things easier for him. To grease the skids of Santa's sleigh, as it were. Some do trivial things to help, others do very substantial, very important things. Even us Helpers don't know who all the other Helpers are. No one does, except him—Santa. He likes lists, as you know, and I'm sure he's got a very detailed list of all the Helpers in his computer at the Pole."

"Santa didn't always need so many Helpers," says Steger. "This big Helpers network is only the latest of a lot of adjustments."

Steger explains, as Santa Claus explained it to him: "In the old days, Santa could pretty much do it himself. His maps were way ahead of anyone else's—just look at

"Frankly, I'm surprised the experiment worked. When Oran approached me, I thought he was out of his mind."

– JOE MEHLING,
photographer

'The Norway Map'—and his sleigh was the finest vehicle on earth. Santa's operation was just about as sophisticated and well oiled as anything, anywhere. In fact, in the Middle Ages he had time on his hands. He was finishing early each year—three, four o'clock in the morning. So he started to play around with refinements. But many of these didn't work out. For instance, rather than keep racing back to the Pole, he started goofing with elves shuttling the presents to him in small sleighs with apprentice reindeer, transferring the gifts in midair at supersonic speeds. Well, as you might imagine, there was a *lot* of spillage. Dolls were raining all over Australia one year. Santa gave up that idea.

"And just as he did, he found all of a sudden that he didn't have quite so much time left over any more. The world was getting to be a bigger place. More people in Europe, many more in Africa. More places colonized. And, sadly, more and more and more poor people. The poor are the ones dearest to Santa, the ones who need him most.

"So he abandoned all his newfangled ideas and concentrated on becoming an absolute master of the task at hand."

In order to stay on top of the game, Claus developed ever more sophisticated routes of flight. He added more retreats to the Pole for gifts, so he was never traveling in an overburdened state. Speed was the key, and each year he would tweak this or that, and squeeze a few more miles per hour from his sleigh. In approximately 1750, Claus seized upon a brilliant idea: He would work east-to-west (following the sun) *and* would start each leg near the South Pole, where late December is sunniest. The flight plan became a zigzag on top of a zigzag, with tangents and U-turns thrown in for good measure.

The Mehling-Young Speed Test, 1991

The Concept: *Oran Young helps Santa Claus plot his Christmas Eve flight routes—crunching distances, wind speeds and other statistics in Institute computers. Therefore, he knows with some precision where Claus is positioned at any given time on the big night. For instance, over New Hampshire.*

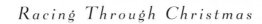

Fig. 1

Fig. 2

The Execution: *Young and photographer Joe Mehling floodlit the Dartmouth green to allow for Mehling to use a reasonably fast film for night shooting. Setting the lens at ⅟₂₅₀th of a second, Mehling let his camera run for nearly ten straight minutes. At that point, something streaked across the sky.*

The Evidence: *When the film was developed, these three frames—recorded over ³⁄₂₅₀ths of a second—were among thousands of images. By dividing time into distance traveled (Young measured it at 1.9 miles, using local landmarks), a velocity was arrived at: Santa Claus speeds along at 650 miles per second.*

Fig. 3

But each time he conquered the earth, it changed again. More people in America, new countries forged, new lands discovered. Small islands were settled, and ones that were sparsely populated—Oahu in Hawaii,

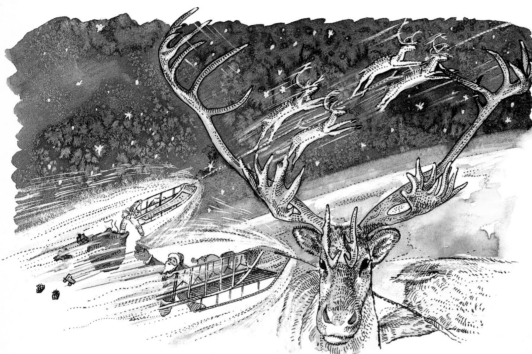

for instance, not to mention everything else in the Pacific—experienced exponential growth. Places where Claus once stopped for rest were now towns, and towns were now cities. Cities were "metropolitan areas" a hundred miles wide.

And then, even as balloons were appearing over the Pole and the sleds of European adventurers were sliding over the Arctic ice cap, a new and troublesome presence was visited upon The Christmas Mission. The airplane.

THAT WAS THE CLINCHER," says Steger as he stirs embers in the hearth. "He said so. Up until then, he figured he could handle whatever came along in the way of population growth or whatever else. Because, you see, the sky was his highway,

Santa Claus has overcome manmade hazards, and at least one blunder of his own.

and he had it to himself. He was more clever than the rest of us, so he could stay a step ahead. That's what he thought, anyway.

"And then, one Christmas Eve early in this century, he's zooming along, singing and having a wonderful night of it. The weather's crisp, and the stars are out. He's coming in for a landing in Washington, D.C., which is always his first stop in the United States. He's coming in and— *brrrrrp!*—this little plane zips right in front of Dasher's nose, and the whole team rears up. He lost a bunch of presents on that one.

"Well, he found out what it was soon enough, but he didn't do anything about it right away. It was a few years later when airplanes were everywhere that he realized he needed help. He decided to reach out, and ever since then he has done so, on a case-by-case basis.

"No one, not even Santa, can succeed alone. When times got tough for him, he asked for help. It's to everyone's credit that he found it."

THE AID THAT HAS BEEN extended to The Christmas Mission in our time is a story worth telling. It is the story of Santa's team. This team includes nine famous reindeer, of course, but also the much less well known Helpers who, upon being summoned by the elf, have excitedly, happily answered the call. It is a story that reflects well on our world.

CHART of EVIDENCE

EUROPE

ICELAND & GREENLAND (THROUGHOUT HISTORY) RUNES AND RUINS ATTRIBUTED TO ELF NATION

VICTORIA ISLAND 1898 – ANDREE MISSIVE WASHES ASHORE

LONDON – 1919 – TRACKS & SCAT FOUND ON BAKER STREET, DETERMINED TO BE OF REINDEER

PORTRUSH, IRELAND, 1963 MYSTERIOUS PHOTOGRAPH SHOWING REINDEER FLIGHT IS FOUND IN PUB

PARIS – 1970 PIECE OF SLED RUNNER FOUND AT BASE OF EIFFEL TOWER

NORTH AMERICA

LABRADOR – (THROUGHOUT HISTORY) ARCHAEOLOGICAL EVIDENCE OF ELVES' EXODUS FOUND

NEW YORK 1809 – WASHINGTON IRVING PUBLISHES RESEARCH ON SANTA CLAUS

DURANGO, COLO. – 1847 – THE LARKIN SIGHTING

HIBBING, MINN. 1967 SMALL PIECE OF ANTLER FOUND ON WEATHERVANE

HANOVER, N.H. 1991 – THE MEHLING-YOUNG SPEED TEST PROVES SLEIGH VELOCITY MAKES TRIP POSSIBLE

CENTRAL & SOUTH AMERICA

6TH CENTURY PANAMANIAN CAVE ART DEPICTS REINDEER, ARCTIC ANIMAL

BRAZIL, 1905 REINDEER TRACKS FOUND IN AMAZONIAN MUD

ARGENTINA, 1930s GUILLAUMET FINDS A RE-SUPPLY CACHE IN THE ANDES

1980 ECUADORIAN MOLA WITH DEER MOTIF FOUND IN MARKET

ASIA

MIDDLE EAST FIRST CENTURIES A.D. REPORTS OF ANONYMOUS WINTER GIFT-GIVER

10TH CENTURY BUDDHIST MONKS BEGIN WRITING OF MTN. SPIRITS' UNREST IN DECEMBER

SANTA FIRST VISITS JAPAN, 1324 (STEGER TESTIMONY)

INDIA 1943 ELEPHANT TUSK ENGRAVED WITH SLEIGH AND REINDEER FOUND IN TAJ MAHAL

NEPAL/TIBET, 1953 HILLARY WITNESSES TENZING'S OFFERING

AFRICA

NATAL, 1800s TRANSLATIONS OF BANTU TELL OF ZULU SIGHTING

TANZANIA, 1919 CACHE FOUND NEAR KIBO SUMMIT OF KILIMANJARO 19,317 ft.

SAHARA, 1933 MITTEN FOUND IN DESERT (REPORTEDLY)

EGYPT, 1941 HIEROGLYPHS OF REINDEER DISCOVERED IN TOMBS

AUSTRALIA

EASTERN AUSTRALIA 1770 – JAMES COOK EXPLORES COAST – WRITES OF ABORIGINES TELLING OF FLYING DEER

HOBART, DEC. 24, 1875 – PRISONERS IN THE PENAL COLONY SERVED EXTRA FOOD ANONYMOUSLY

AYERS ROCK, CENTRAL AUSTRALIA, 1922 ABORIGINAL ROCK PAINTINGS INVOLVING FLYING REINDEER FOUND IN CAVES

QUEENSLAND, 1945 KANGAROOS SPOTTED CARRYING PACKAGES – DOLLS, GOODS – IN THEIR POUCHES

PART FOUR

Eight Tiny Reindeer (Plus One)

Santa's Starting Team and His Helpers

THEIR NAMES WERE bestowed by Santa Claus himself—in the elfin language, of course. "Santa said it was easy," says Will Steger. "Each reindeer has a very distinctive personality that showed itself early in life—hundreds and hundreds of years ago. For instance, Dasher was a sprite when he was a kid. He was hyperactive."

Cupid in Love

Rudolph

Dasher

Blitzen & Donder

"THE ENGINES"

AND NOW, STEGER POINTS OUT, Dasher's job is to get the team off the mark quickly. He digs his forepaws into the ice, he grunts, and he just *goes*. Apparently he spends all of November practicing his starts.

"Comet, a small deer even for a Peary, can race all night long," Steger continues. "He can run forever at high speeds. I saw him training casually at the Pole— he was the only one of the elite eight that wasn't sleeping when I was there. He was doing this light workout—not even approaching supersonic speeds, just traipsing across the ice fields—and he looked like a marathoner with the speed of a sprinter. On the night itself, he gives the team a boost whenever anyone starts to lag."

Steger laughs lightly. "I asked Santa how Cupid got his name," he says. "He just smiled. I guess Cupid sometimes causes problems during the off-season, because he's constantly getting distracted—falling for this young deer, then that one. It's hard to keep Cupid focused. What a lot of people don't know is that Cupid is a male. Dancer, Prancer and Vixen are female. Blitzen and Donder, both males, are the biggest deer. They're the engine for the team, they're the power. They each go about three hundred pounds—oversized, for a Peary. They're like the offensive linemen on a football team or

The Russian Peary built a brilliant stairway to the stars.

the lead rowers on an eight-man crew. They're set back near the sleigh, to push and prod the others.

"Yes, Santa named them all. He said the only one he didn't name was Rudolph, who came from a Peary family in what is now Russia. Rudolph had already been named by his parents when Santa discovered him. You see, Rudolph—as opposed to the others, all of whom were handpicked as youngsters by Santa more than two thousand years ago—wasn't earmarked for the team. He wasn't raised to help Santa. It just happened that way because of one extraordinary circumstance.

"Nowadays, of course, Santa says he doesn't know how he ever got along without Rudolph."

And yet he did for nearly 500 years. It was 463 when the snow came to Europe like it never had on December 24th, and never would again. The idea to use Rudolph that night was Claus's and Claus's alone, and turned out to be a stroke of genius.

He had found Rudolph only two years earlier. In 461 he had just finished delivering gifts of food to the Yakut people of Siberia, and he was back at the Pole filling up with presents for the Huns, who had been behaving better since the death of the tyrannical Attila eight

LOS ANGELES 1995

BAD VISIBILITY   LONDON 1850

NEW YORK ~ 1910

years earlier.[6] "It's awfully foggy down there tonight," he told his polar assistants. "It's warm, so there's an extremely thick fog. We'll be all right, but landing's going to be awfully tough."

The 5th century knew of fire, of course, but not of any kind of unnatural light. So imagine Claus's astonishment when his team came hurtling out of the high altitudes down into the fog, slowed for safety and then suddenly picked up a beam of light shining heavenward like a beacon. "To say I was surprised," Claus told Steger, "is to say the obvious. I remember Dasher looked back at me as if to ask, 'What is this?'"

It was the light from Rudolph's nose, and Claus steered his sleigh down the beam, descending the brilliant staircase with all the beauty, serenity and elegance of a bride. Why the young Peary was standing in the center of a village quite near what is now Moscow, silently calling to his kin-deer, has never been explained, and probably never will be. But there are sixth, seventh and eighth senses at work in the world of Santa Claus, and almost certainly there was some measure of communication between the several Peary in the air and the solitary Peary on the ground.

THAT VERY NIGHT Claus asked Rudolph if he wanted to help the team. Who could refuse? So while Santa and just six deer worked the region that is now the southern Ukraine, Prancer and Vixen gave Rudolph a crash course in flying. The youth had some natural talent and even more potential, and by the time

"Could Santa Claus succeed today without computers and radar? That's a very good question."

– KEN CAMPBELL,
technician and Helper

the Christmas missionaries returned to the European Plain with an empty sleigh, Rudolph had been sufficiently schooled to follow the team up and away, and back to the Pole.

That was the extent of Rudolph's participation in 461. In 462 the sky over most of the earth was cloudless, and the eight-deer team had little problem making the rounds without him. But Claus knew he had hit on something special in Rudolph. The elf had often thought about glowing animals: Certain lizards glowed, several marsupials in the southern hemisphere glowed. Why couldn't a reindeer glow?

Then he found Rudolph, and soon—a little too soon, perhaps—he had an opportunity to find out whether this anointed Peary could perform in the unique way Claus hoped and dreamed he could perform.

FROM WHAT I CAN glean from ancient records and charts," says Ken Campbell, a meteorologist with Weather Services Corporation of Lexington, Massachusetts, "four-sixty-three was just about the worst Christmas Eve you can imagine. England got four feet of snow in a day, and though the winds were worse there than elsewhere, the continent got even more snow—five feet in France, perhaps that much in Rome. It was unbelievable. It was an Armageddon of snow and wind. It made the word 'blizzard' inadequate."

Steger says that Santa Claus not only remembers Rudolph's first big year, but he talks about it often. "Santa loves to tell stories, which is good since he has more and better stories to tell than just about anyone," says Steger. "The Rudolph story is his absolute favorite.

[6] In the 5th century, the Huns were centered in a region not far from where Moscow is today. (The Russian capital had not yet been founded.)

"Until then, he had been training young Rudolph to follow the team or stay alongside as the sleigh went along—not to lead. Santa figured a general cast of light from that nose would be enough to guide the way through any weather, and that perhaps Rudolph could sit with him in the sleigh. But when Santa saw 'The Winter o' Sixty-three,' as he still calls it, well, he knew Rudolph needed to be up front.

"Santa had already gone out once that night, and for the first time ever had come back without being able to land. It was clear that what he needed was a headlight. That's what Rudolph was, the world's first headlight."

Rudolph was also in trouble. He was harnessed at the front of the squad ahead of Dasher and Dancer. Claus's team was supportive but concerned. Rudolph had a prodigious talent in his nose, but his flying skills were suspect, his mettle untested, his strength below average. Could he lead the team in a slight breeze, never mind a raging storm?

All Claus knew, as he landed back at the Pole with

Weather Services Corporation monitors training missions for Claus, and works with air-traffic control to clear Peary airspace.

undelivered gifts, was that he had to try. And so, with a hesitant "hup, *hup,*" he urged the team up, Rudolph leading. They ascended slowly, and as they went this slightest

Peary was blown side to side. At high altitudes—Claus cruises at 26,000 feet on the longer carries, 35,000 over mountainous terrain—Rudolph was steady and firm, but as soon as the sleigh descended again into the thicker atmosphere, the little reindeer was buffeted by every wind. Every wind *except* the worst wind.

THAT WAS THE STRANGE THING. Rudolph would be thrown left, right, up and down—he'd be all over the place, with the glow from his nose whipping around the night sky as if a drunkard was searching with a flashlight. But then the team would enter the thick stuff, and Rudolph would turn into a rock. When the going got truly tough, the tough Russian deer got going. In the worst gales, Rudolph would res- olutely streamline his small body, becoming a satellite of firmness and force. He would thrust his nose forth and make straight for the target. He could not only show the way but also see it.

"Santa told me that many times over the years he would steer one way, but Rudolph would take him anoth- er," recalls Steger. "Now, Santa had never, ever been over- ruled by a deer. Not even the sagacious Donder had questioned his judgment. But in these cases Rudolph was seeing things that Santa just couldn't see from the sleigh. Santa was slow to realize this. But gradually—and grudgingly, because he's a pretty proud elf—Santa yielded whenever Rudolph was at the helm."

In our time, Rudolph has become the most famous reindeer of all, a star of song and network television.

WHAT WOULD BECOME RUDOLPH'S long history of routine courage and fortitude began in that awful year of 463. It was already nearly midnight when the new traveling squad made its way south over Iceland toward London, and then plunged into the maelstrom. Claus was astonished when Rudolph kicked into gear as soon as the sleigh was engulfed by the blizzard. He watched the youngster take it upon his slen- der shoulders to pull The Mission through. Innately sensing what was necessary, Rudolph shone his 1.2-million- lumen nose here, then switched it over there.[7] He flew like Santa had never seen a reindeer fly before. Rudolph hit each landing perfectly, including one on the top of a steepled cathe- dral in Rome. Claus still considers that the most deftly executed of his many billion landings. "Morluv said that Santa talks about it all the time—that and everything else that happened in 463," says Steger. "Morluv makes fun of him for it. 'Remember

7 The brightness estimate is just that—an estimate. Steger says Santa Claus equated the nose's effectiveness to that of "a hundred lighthouses."

DISTANCE NEEDED FOR EMERGENCY LANDING

TOWER

AN EMERGENCY
LANDING DURING
A CHRISTMAS TYPHOON
IN THE PACIFIC OCEAN

when Rudolph, in '63, found that church in Rome and....' Morluv and the others love to tease Santa about being— well, a little windy. But, really, I mean, who has better stories to tell than that guy? Like I said, he's a storyteller. Whose stories would you rather hear? Name one person."

The Mission of 463 lasted until nearly eleven in the morning, but no one in the world noticed—the storm was still so bad on the 25th, you couldn't tell if it was night or day. Thereafter, it was clear that Rudolph would be called into service whenever bad weather threatened. He would train constantly, and go if needed.

This was the way it was, for more than a millennium. Then, in the early 19th century, pollution over London and other heavily populated cities forced Claus to use Rudolph each year in certain areas. The Russian reindeer hasn't had a year off since. If you look past blizzards and other weather vagaries, it's accurate to say that Rudolph's workload has increased precisely to the degree that smog has increased. He now leads several legs of The Mission each year, though never works a thirty-one-hour night like the others. "As I said, Rudolph is not a big deer," says Steger, "so Santa doesn't want to just hitch him to the team and use him for every trip. Even as it is, Rudolph stays in recovery until nearly June each year. He's a small deer with a big heart."

"Santa once joked that if he didn't have help, New York City would take him half the night."

– AL ROKER, *meteorologist and Helper*

HOW DOES CLAUS KNOW which jaunts—besides Los Angeles, Mexico City and other obvious ones—should be Rudolph jaunts? He used to rely on intuition. Now he uses that, and a lot of science.

"Santa stays in touch with several meteorologists worldwide," says Campbell. "He calls them often in December, and his calls become more frequent as Christmas approaches. Just before he takes off, he calls each of us. We supply data concerning cloud cover, wind patterns, high and low pressure areas. From this, he plans which trips Rudolph will lead.

"I'll give you a couple of examples. Rudolph almost always has to do the Southern California swing because of the smog. But Rudolph only has to do the Australian trip if there's a typhoon down there. You see? Santa loves it if he can spare Rudolph the Southern Hemisphere runs, because the big distances tire the little fellow out.

"Rudolph's heaviest years were 1914 through '18, and 1938 through '45. When the world is at war, Santa's job becomes as difficult as it is necessary. With bombs bursting up there and down below, Rudolph is needed to cut through the smoke."

Campbell, for his part, was first needed by Claus in 1987. "People here at Weather Services had helped plot weather for Will Steger's trip, and I guess Steger told Santa about our computers, our data gathering abilities and so forth. One day, he just called. It's funny, I was on the phone with the guy—*and I didn't doubt who he was.* He's just the most sincere, most obviously honest fellow you've ever talked to. I'm proud to be a Helper. Who wouldn't be?"

Campbell is not the only weatherman Helper. The big picture that he provides with his global-reach instruments is embellished by the local view. Regional weather-watchers worldwide, professionals and amateurs alike, are in touch with the North Pole. "I've been helping for twelve years now," says Al Roker, the weatherman on NBC's *Today* show. He files crucial reports from that

most variable and dangerous of places, New York City. "Santa *does* like New York," says Roker. "He told me so. He said it gives him everything. We've got the needy, the world's many populations, the races, the unity of people in a common setting trying to get along. That's what New York's all about, and that's what he's all about. He said, 'New York is like me—big and always awake.'"

Roker continues: "But no, he doesn't find New York easy. It's a challenge for him. The buildings make things tough, and the way nor'easters sweep down off New England has messed him up many a time.

"He wants to make sure New York goes smoothly each year. He doesn't want to miss one kid in New York, especially with so many poor. But he doesn't want to waste time here, either. That would throw off his schedule. So he phones constantly on the 23rd and even the 24th. I work with Ken Campbell on that. Ken gives Santa the approach from the northeast, the landing profile from Connecticut. I give him the local knowledge. For instance, the weather that we experienced here a week earlier could impact the slide-ratio on New York rooftops. They might still be slick with ice, they might be dry, they might be snow-covered. There are a lot of rooftops in Manhattan, and if I can help Santa do this town in a half-hour or less, then I feel like a hero."

K EN CAMPBELL is a Helper, Al Roker is a Helper. On Kauai in the Hawaiian Islands, Lisa Patrick is also a Helper. And although she is a Helper you would expect to hear about, you still might laugh at the part she plays. She is a chimney sweep.

"Here's the chimney sweep joke," she says. "It's a dirty job, but somebody's got to do it." It's not as dirty a job in Hawaii as it is in the industrial cities, but come December 24th, it is an essential job. "Does Santa come down every chimney?" asks Patrick. "No. Of course not. I'll tell you what I tell my three-year-old daughter Michaela, which happens to be the truth. Santa is a housebreaker. Basically, that's what he is. He comes through an open window, a door ajar, a loose floorboard in the trailer, a dog's door in the kitchen. He's small and fast, so the chimney is the surest way. That's why the chimney has become the classic image— because he always tries a chimney first. But if the flue is shut, he does what he can. He does what he has to.

"I'm a Helper because he asked me to be. My husband and I were home one night, I was pregnant with Michaela at the time. The phone rang, and it was him. I didn't believe it at first, and I still don't know who put him in touch with me. But have you ever talked to him? He's got *such* a sweet voice. So persuasive. You don't hear enough voices like that.

"Eventually, I believed it was him. He asked me if I could leave the flue open in the chimneys that I swept. I remember his concern. He said, 'I wouldn't ask this of an Alaskan because of the cold, but I figured in Hawaii. . . .' I said, 'Sure.' Ever since, he's been using nothing but chimneys on Kauai."

"He's a tough bird. I asked him if he wanted a windshield on that sled of his, and he just laughed."

– MELISSA FRANKLIN, *physicist and Helper*

T HERE ARE WEATHERMEN with radar helping Santa Claus, there are sweeps with brooms, and there are many others in between. There is a physicist—at Harvard, no less—whose name is Dr. Melissa Franklin. A Canadian by birth ("We're so proud that Santa's first North American settlement was in Goose Bay"), Franklin has been teaching at the august institution since 1985. "I really haven't done much to help Santa, just a few simple calculations. As The Mission became more complex and the speeds faster, Santa needed to determine an optimal weight for the sleigh. He wanted to know what was the most cargo he could carry without

the time and the right computer software. But I was pleased to be asked."

So was Oran Young, Helper Extraordinaire. "Like Melissa, I think of myself as one of Santa's Eggheads," he says. "I get the sense he was happier when he could do this thinking and plotting for himself. But he realizes that in

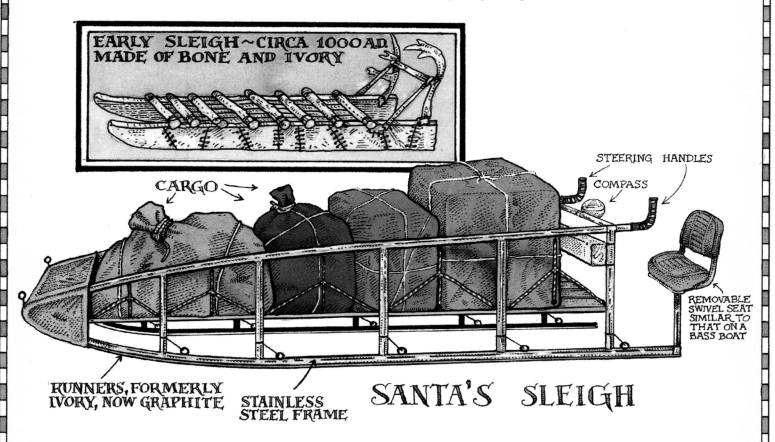

EARLY SLEIGH ~ CIRCA 1000 A.D.
MADE OF BONE AND IVORY

CARGO

STEERING HANDLES

COMPASS

REMOVABLE
SWIVEL SEAT
SIMILAR TO
THAT ON A
BASS BOAT

RUNNERS, FORMERLY
IVORY, NOW GRAPHITE

STAINLESS
STEEL FRAME

SANTA'S SLEIGH

sacrificing speed. I did wind-tunnel tests on a sleigh just like his. He gave me the dimensions, and we built a model here at the university. Then we computed the drag coefficient—how the wind passes most smoothly over the sleigh. Then I crunched some numbers in the computer, and gave him a figure. If the reindeer are averaging under three hundred pounds each and Santa has watched the cookies—one-fifty is his best weight, and that's a strong one-fifty since he's barely three feet tall—then he can pack more than a ton of loot on each trip."

Dr. Franklin is being modest when she adds, "Anyone could have done the math, really. Santa himself, if he had

the modern age he needs the help of the eggheads."

Young serves as a coordinator. His Institute of Arctic Studies has long been involved with the airlines in helping regulate traffic flow over the North Pole. "The increase in circumpolar flights has been exponential since 1970," he says. "The world has become a much smaller place with faster and faster planes, and now it's a short hop from London to Hong Kong—over the top.

"So what I do is, I talk to the major airlines. I negotiate a one-night moratorium of their great circumpolar routes. Everyone cooperates, and I think everyone's happy to. They understand the problem. I mean, Santa's banging in

SANTA'S CHRISTMAS EVE

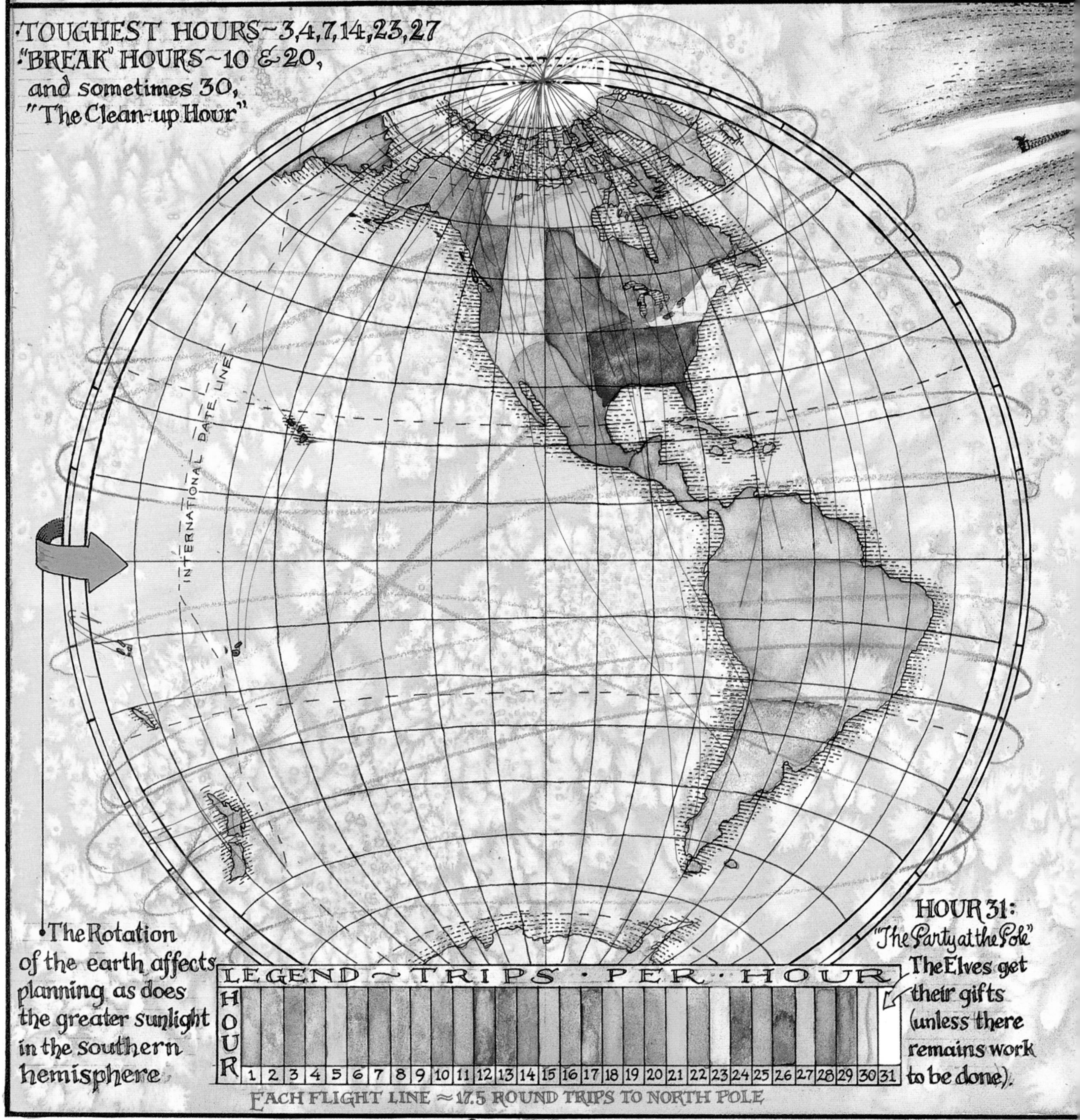

TOUGHEST HOURS ~ 3,4,7,14,23,27
"BREAK" HOURS ~ 10 & 20,
and sometimes 30,
"The Clean-up Hour"

INTERNATIONAL DATE LINE

• The Rotation
of the earth affects
planning as does
the greater sunlight
in the southern
hemisphere

HOUR 31:
"The Party at the Pole"
The Elves get
their gifts
(unless there
remains work
to be done).

LEGEND ~ TRIPS · PER · HOUR

HOUR

| 1 | 2 | 3 | 4 | 5 | 6 | 7 | 8 | 9 | 10 | 11 | 12 | 13 | 14 | 15 | 16 | 17 | 18 | 19 | 20 | 21 | 22 | 23 | 24 | 25 | 26 | 27 | 28 | 29 | 30 | 31 |

EACH FLIGHT LINE ≈ 17.5 ROUND TRIPS TO NORTH POLE

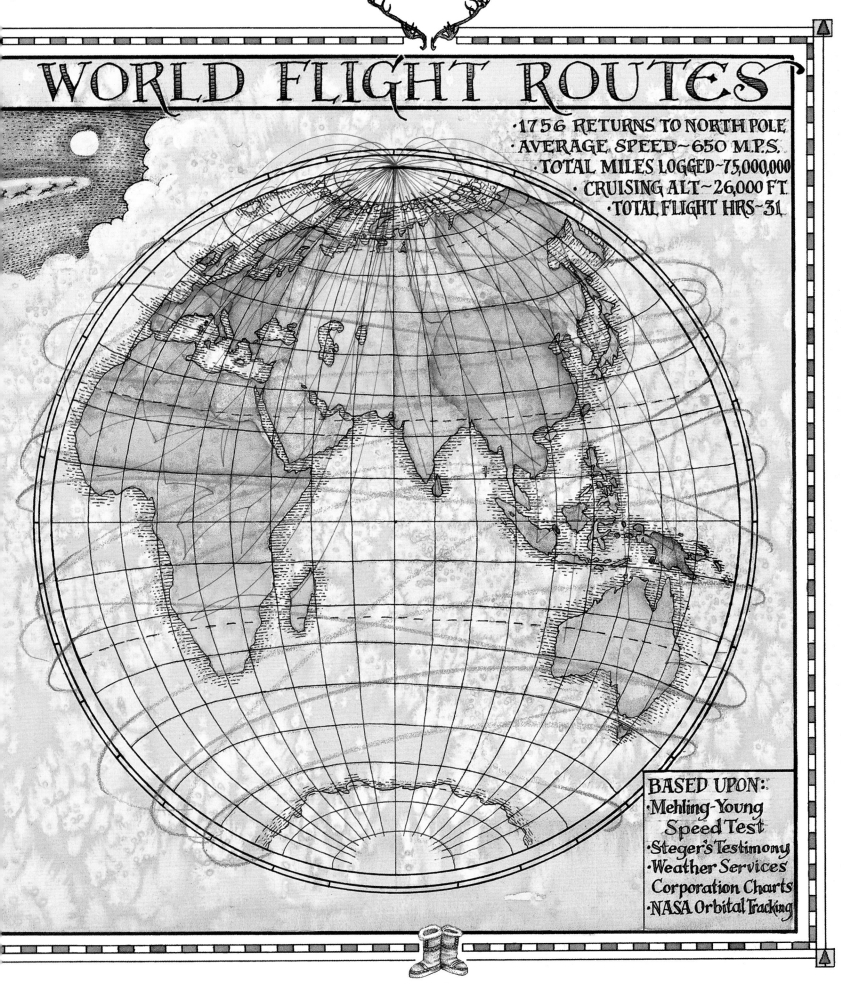

WORLD FLIGHT ROUTES

- 1756 RETURNS TO NORTH POLE
- AVERAGE SPEED ~ 650 M.P.S.
- TOTAL MILES LOGGED ~ 75,000,000
- CRUISING ALT ~ 26,000 FT.
- TOTAL FLIGHT HRS ~ 31

BASED UPON:
- Mehling-Young Speed Test
- Steger's Testimony
- Weather Services Corporation Charts
- NASA Orbital Tracking

and out of the Pole all night long, and if these big birds are zipping around at 30,000 feet, there's eventually going to be a problem, a terrible accident. So everyone clears the air over the Pole for thirty-one hours. And this is not just a U.S. thing. Aeroflot cooperates and China Air cooperates, Qantas cooperates and Air France cooperates. This annual moratorium stands, really, as a testament to the kind of man Santa is."

Former President of the United States George Bush confirms and concurs. "It's just as Oran says, we do it because of who Santa is, what he does, what he stands for," says Bush, speaking from his office in Houston. "I didn't know one blessed thing about this before I got to the White House. Then during my first term as President— probably about October of 1989—I was presented with this longstanding agreement that all Presidents sign-off on each year. This was the international accord that directs our airlines to watch themselves, and to clear that airspace up there, up there, up there over the Pole. I didn't think for a minute, not a minute. I looked at the thing and I said, 'For Santa Claus? Sure.' I signed immediately. He's a great ambassador for peace and fellowship in this world. America absolutely *should* be in the business of encouraging his work."

❧

"I told Bill Clinton that signing the Santa Claus clause was just about the nicest thing he'd get to do each year."

– GEORGE BUSH,
*former U.S. President
and Helper*

PRESIDENTS ARE HELPERS, and so are hobbyists. Robert Andreas of Croton-on-Hudson, a town just up the river from New York City, is a copy editor in Manhattan. By night, he is an amateur astronomer of high reputation. "I've been doing star charts for Santa for five or six years now, and I've never worked for a sweeter person. It's basically stuff

that Santa himself used to do—advanced celestial navigation and so forth. He could do it still, he certainly has the expertise—just look at that world map he drew, the one they found in Norway in 1654. But he's just gotten so busy that he now farms out some of these smaller, niggling jobs.

"I got brought into the network by Oran Young. The Helpers quite often tip Santa off to someone else, and then he calls. I'll be honest with you, my biggest contribution to The Mission was probably putting Santa in touch with a veterinarian. Her name's Joan Regan. She's down in Pennsylvania, and you should call her. She's got a lovely tale to tell. Of all the Helpers, I think she has probably helped the most. Call on her—You've got to hear Joan's story."

❧

THE CALL IS MADE, and Dr. Regan of Haverford tells the tale: "Well, how it came about was, Bob asked if I'd ever worked with reindeer. I laughed and said we didn't have a lot of reindeer in greater Philadelphia. He said, 'Well you might have one tomorrow.'

"When I awoke, there was a Peary caribou in my backyard, holding its left foreleg off the ground. I hadn't the foggiest idea how it had gotten there. It was like the unicorn-in-the-garden story.

"I went out, and found that there was a note attached to its antlers. I've saved the note, of course. I'll read it to you. It says, 'Dear Dr. Regan, My name is Donder, and it seems I have hurt my leg while running. The vets where I come from are very capable, but they work mostly with herbal medicines, and my handler says he believes surgery is needed. Time is of the essence. Could you help me? It is important to me—

and to others—that this injury be treated properly. And so my trainer has sent me to you, as you come very highly recommended. I would appreciate it if you could help me. And so would my owner.'

"That's the whole note. No signature, no hoof print.

"So, anyway, I went to work on the leg. I ultra-sounded it, and found that the injury wasn't as serious as the trainer had feared. Trainers have been known to overreact. The Peary had tendinitis, and this responded to antiinflammatory medication and a bit of rest. I waited for the owner to call, or to come over and pick up his reindeer. No one ever did.

"That's it. End of story.

"Somehow, this deer named Donder got out of the backyard pen, and I never saw him again."

Regan pauses, then smiles.

"There is a postscript," she says. "I think it was perhaps September, maybe even October when I treated Donder. I waited patiently through November, but I never got any payment—no check in the mail, no token of thanks, not even a letter or card of acknowledgement. And then, on Christmas morning, I came downstairs and under my tree was a little reindeer, and it had a splint on its left foreleg. Out in the back-

yard was an ice-sculpture that looked just like Donder.

"Now do you suppose...."

Christmas, 1987

Dr. Regan took a snapshot of "Donder" in '87. This gift now adorns the mantle above her fireplace.

OF COURSE YOU DO. And so does Joan Regan—*Dr.* Joan Regan. And so does Melissa Franklin—*Dr.* Melissa Franklin. And so does Robert Andreas and Oran Young and Lisa Patrick and Al Roker and Tony Vecchio and Ken Campbell and Will Steger and Phil Cronenwett and Einar Gustavsson and Bil Gilbert and, yes, even former President George W. Bush and Sir Edmund Hillary themselves—and anyone else who has bothered to think about Santa Claus.

Of course you suppose it is him.

And this brings a smile to your face, as it does to the face of Joan Regan.

But *why* is it him?

What have we done to deserve him?

"That is something," says Joan Regan, "that I wonder about each and every night. It is something I mull over as I lie in bed. It's a mystery. But it's a nice mystery, and whatever the answer is doesn't really matter. Because whatever it is, it makes me feel warm inside. It helps me to sleep peacefully. It gives me great hope. It makes me want to wake up, tomorrow."

Like Down on a Thistle, Evermore

Work That Never Ends

ASHER, Dancer, Prancer and Vixen are not immortal. Comet, Cupid, the now-healed Donder and Blitzen are special but aging deer. Rudolph too. He's a real Peary, with the aches and pains of a real Peary. You should see him each December 26th—he is one sore animal.

They are getting older, yes, but these special reindeer of the North Pole count time in a different way than we do. Consider: The Big Eight of Santa's squad have been a team for 2,000 years—with Rudolph, they've been a team for 1,500—but it is clear, from the testimony of Steger and others, that they will remain a team throughout your lifetime, your children's lifetimes and all the lifetimes of your children's children's grandchildren. For a thousand more trips—and more than that—Santa Claus will drive the same famous group of reindeer. "He told me so," says Will Steger. "And I believe everything that he told me, without question."

Think back, with Steger's testimony in mind, to where our search began. Do you remember the vision that the ancient Inuit of Kuujjuaq saw outlined against the moon, the one captured in leather with a hunting knife? That is exactly the same vision you can spy out your midnight window, if you are very, very lucky—and the reindeer are in glide, traveling very, very slowly. You and your descendants and theirs and theirs. What a thought that is! What an opportunity each of us has.

"He did say," Steger adds, "that thousands of years in the future, he'll have to replace his legendary deer. One by one, they'll be too old. At that point, some phenomenal flier from the training group will be given the nod, and will be hitched to the Christmas sleigh. I wouldn't want to be one of those youngsters, not on the maiden voyage. What pressure! Can you imagine being the one who replaces Dasher? Dancer?"

When the day finally does come, the famous old deer who have performed so nobly will undoubtedly enjoy a serene retirement. They will silently impart advice to the new kids on the team, then just lie around the stable. They'll spend their golden years remembering all those bygone Christmas Eves, all the adventures, all the places, all the glories. The fur near their antlers will slowly go gray. They'll watch The Christmas Mission lifting off, and tears will roll softly down toward their noses.

But not yet, and not soon. The same Santa Claus express that our world has come to love will be on the job for a long time yet. The team's members have, as we have seen, learned to cope with our modern times. They have taken on the heavier and heavier burden of serving an ever more populous planet. They have—always, every year—served as perfectly and generously as they have served quietly and modestly. These small, strong, silent deer: They are the best this earth can offer.

The End

Credits

MANY THANKS are extended to the following contributors of artifacts and photography, listed by page. Pages 13, 14, 16, 40, 41 (2), 42, 44, 63, 67: The Stefansson Collection at Baker Library/Dartmouth College; 20, 26, 29, 73: Joe Mehling; 25: Leif Ericsson courtesy of Richard D. Bond, "Columbus Discovers America" courtesy of the U.S. Naval Academy Museum; 28: courtesy of Carlton Plummer; 30: courtesy of F. Forrester Church; 31: "St. Nicholas of Bari," 1472 by Carlo Crivelli © The Cleveland Museum of Art, gift of the Hanna Fund; 33: "Another Stocking to Fill" and "Santa Claus's Mail" by Thomas Nast, the Irving portrait from The Bettmann Archive; 34: courtesy of Regina Barreca; 35: William H. Johnson; 38: Per Breiehagan; 39, 46, 47, 55, back cover: Will Steger/Black Star; 48: Tony Stone Images; 52: courtesy of Jeff Blumenfeld; 58: Dana Smith; 60: courtesy of Bil Gilbert; 64: Jim Brandenburg/Minden Pictures; 68, back cover: Andrew Cornaga/Photosport, New Zealand; 69: The Royal Geographical Society, London (2); 71: Ned Gillete Photography (2); 72: Kathy Rae Chapman; 80: courtesy Weather Services Corporation; 81: Tony Stone Images; 82: ©Rankin-Bass Productions; 84, back cover: courtesy of NBC-TV Network; 86: courtesy of Melissa Franklin; 90, back cover: Michael Moore.

I.F: MARIRY

SANTA
EVIDENCE
COLLECTION
#15.1147
0.0. NORWAY
1654

Santa's Flight Map
found in Norway, 1654